THE

TOTAL

PACKAGE

Keys to Acquiring Wealth
and Walking in Divine Health

George B. Thompson

and

Aaron D. Lewis

The Total Package: Keys to Acquiring Wealth and Walking in Divine Health

George B. Thompson
P.O. Box 90761
Los Angeles, CA 90009
Trainingmillionaires.com
thompsongb@aol.com

Pastor Aaron D. Lewis
P.O. Box 8286
Manchester, CT 06040-0286
Fog135@aol.com
Fax: (860) 290-8291

ISBN 1-880809-21-4
Printed in the United States of America
© 2003 by George B. Thompson and Aaron D. Lewis

Legacy Publishers International
1301 South Clinton Street
Denver, CO 80247
www.legacypublishersinternational.com

Cover design by: Nikki Braun

1 2 3 4 5 6 7 8 9 10 11 / 09 08 07 06 05 04 03

Advance Praise for
The Total Package

In **The Total Package**, Thompson and Lewis speak to a person's body, soul and spirit, using a holistic approach, while activating the mind skills needed in order to mine life's opportunities and possibilities. About more than money and medicine, this soul food nourishes a mind-set towards wealth and health.

Rev. Steven D. Johnson, Chief Financial Officer
First AME Church and affiliate corporations
Los Angeles, California

Aaron D. Lewis and George B. Thompson have done a wonderful job clearly articulating the correlation between wealth and health. This book is written in a down-to-earth and straight-to-the-point fashion! It does not merely address the "why(s)" of the situation, but it also gives detailed instructions to accomplish the "how(s)." This book is a must-have for anyone who desires to be "healthy in wealth" and "wealthy in health."

Recording Artists
Bruce Allen & Allen T.D. Wiggins of Allen & Allen
New Release, *Allen & Allen—Impressions*

I am angry at the devil for tricking Christian believers into believing that money doesn't matter and that divine healing is not available to *people today. These lies have so permeated the Body of Christ that many churches and parishioners depict a tattered and torn ragtag army rather than the undefeated Kingdom of God. **The Total Package** was written to rescue you from mediocre thinking and settling for less than God's desires for you. If you can only believe that God truly desires for you to walk in health and wealth, this book is the criterion that will show you how.*

Bishop LeRoy Bailey, Jr., Senior Minister
The First Cathedral, Bloomfield, Connecticut
Author, *A Solid Foundation: Building Your Life From the Ground Up*

The Total Package *provides a biblical map to find the balance between health and wealth in your life. This book properly emphasizes prevention as one of the keys to good health and personal wealth. You will fully understand that health and wealth really cannot be separated!*

Terry Schroeder, D.C.
North Ranch Chiropractic—Chiropractor
Pepperdine University Water Polo Coach
1980, 1984, 1988, 1992, USA Olympian
1984, 1988 Silver Medalist

The Total Package *addresses two critical challenges to experiencing fulfilling and productive lives. This book is an important read on the road to self-actualization.*

Paul C. Hudson, President/CEO
Broadway Federal Bank
10th Largest African-American Bank

This book has a profound and compelling way of telling God's intended purpose for the believer in the spiritual and physical areas of their lives. The discomfort we experience spiritually and physically in our lives is exposed in this book in such a way that if we respond to its call we will relieve our DIS-EASE.

Darrel G. Smith
Save Africa's Children,
a program of Pan-African Children's Fund
Founder/President, SMITH & ASSOCIATES,
an Executive Search Firm

Table of Contents

The purpose of this book is to educate. Many facts set forth in this publication were obtained from sources believed to be reliable, but no guarantee is made with respect to accuracy. Any application of the investment or health advice herein is at the reader's own discretion and risk. If additional financial or health assistance is required, seek the advice of a financial or health professional. The authors and Legacy Publishers International shall have neither liability nor responsibility to any person or entity with respect to loss, damage, or injury caused or alleged to be caused directly or indirectly by the information contained in this book. We assume no responsibility for errors, inaccuracies, omissions, or any inconsistency herein.

George Thompson is available as a keynote speaker at conventions, seminars, and workshops, as well as for organizations wishing to share how anyone can become a "Millionaire in Training." If you would like to discuss a possible speaking engagement, he can be reached at:

George B. Thompson
P.O. Box 90761
Los Angeles, CA 90009
Trainingmillionaires.com
thompsongb@aol.com

You may contact Pastor Aaron D. Lewis for speaking engagements, workshops, and seminars by writing:

Pastor Aaron D. Lewis
P.O. Box 8286
Manchester, CT 06040-0286
Fog135@aol.com
Fax: (860) 290-8291

Acknowledgments

First, I would like to thank God for keeping me safe from dangers seen and unseen. On September 7, 2001, just days before the September 11 attack on America, I was in a near fatal car accident and should not have survived. Because of God's plan for me to help you (His greater purpose), I have life.

I would like to thank and dedicate this book to my mother, Mossie L. Thompson, for her unconditional love which cannot be matched by anyone on earth, and for teaching me the meaning of living in the moment.

To my dad, George B. Thompson, Sr., and my stepmother, Terry, thank you for being consistently dedicated. It has helped me withstand some of the most challenging barriers that I have had to face in life. Both my older brother, Darrell, and my twin sister, Jennifer, have helped me raise my bar of excellence to higher heights in light of all that we have endured together this year.

To my wife, Kimberley Thompson, who is supportive of all my endeavors and completes me in every way, you are the most amazing gift God has given to me.

Thank you, Bishop Charles Blake, the pastor of my church, West Angeles Church of God in Christ, and Bishop Donald Wright of Jabbok Christian Fellowship for your unending support.

The Total Package

I also would like to thank Bishop Andrew C. Turner, Dr. Wanda Davis Turner, and my brother and sister in Christ, Charles and Audrey Gaskin, for being part of my East Coast family. Thank you, Della Woodert, for helping my vision come to pass.

Finally, to my brother in Christ, Pastor Aaron D. Lewis, thank you for your obedience and service to our heavenly Father. This book would not have come to pass without your diligence, faithfulness and gift of writing. God truly has melded our hearts together by His love to complement each other. I thank God that He has brought us together and commissioned us to help unlock the spirit and mind in the members of the Body of Christ and encourage them with the message that they already have *the power to get wealth and walk in divine health.*

George B. Thompson

I feel that it is always befitting to recognize the persons who at some point have added richness to my life. There are those who have continually pursued to be a blessing in my life and have in turn received a perpetual harvest from their sowing. There are others whom God sends for a particular season or purpose. I am sincerely grateful for both.

I thank my wife, Tiwanna, you have been a tremendous blessing as you've allowed me to bounce health and wealth ideas and scenarios off you that have proven to be gems in this piece. Juggling the responsibilities of rearing our five growing children, being actively involved in your own ministry at our church, pioneering a new business, and making the dean's list in your theatre degree this past semester has made me see you in a whole different light. You strip every woman (young and old) of the excuse that settling for mediocrity is an option in life. Go sista!

Acknowledgments

To four of my five children, Eryn, Amber, Judah, and Israel, you inspire me to achieve greatness, if for no other reason, so that you can experience a better life than I did.

I purposely saved my comments about my two-year-old Madonna. Although I would have loved to include her with her other four siblings, her strength to be heard, understood, and respected places her in a class all by herself. She is destined for greatness. Until she arrives at that point, I solicit all your prayers.

To the winning leadership team at *The Family of God*, "Debt-free" Makita Booker, Minister Joanna Brown, Minister Tiwanna "Tee" Lewis, Tanya Richards, and Renair Thorington, thank you for allowing me to stretch you past your comfort zones. It's not over.

To my spiritual father, Bishop LeRoy Bailey, Jr., and Mother Reathie Bailey, by your example, you teach me *love* on a whole new level. Thank you to my beloved friends in ministry who care enough to stay in touch, Evangelist Jack and Frieda Coe, Pastor Gary and Maya Taylor, and Pastor Stenith and Beverly Powell. I thank my brother Morris Lewis who in recent months has made a strong stand to openly love me. It is my brother Kenneth Lewis who first taught me the laws of earning and the complicated science of selling. Thanks to all the covenant members at *The Family of God* who have embraced health and wealth not simply as a book or workshop but rather as a way of life.

My friend George B. Thompson, it has been a wealthy pleasure to work on this project with you.

Finally, I thank God, for He is the one who empowers us to *get wealth and walk in divine health*.

Aaron D. Lewis

The Total Package

Introduction

There are two sad truths that have unfortunately become facts of life. The first truth is that most people in this world do not live quite as long as they had expected to live. Increased pollutants in our air, oil and other contaminants spilling into our drinking water, and massive amounts of chemical preservatives added to our foods are just a few of the many contributing factors that cause disease to enter into our bodies.

Indeed there are several conditions of our environment that we have little control over, yet there are many instances where people can determine what is beneficial to their well-being and fitness, and still they choose not to make conscious healthy decisions. They eat foods on a regular basis that have been proven to reduce life and promote sickness in their bodies. Items such as treadmills, indoor bicycles, and elliptical trainers have become more a part of the household permanent furnishings rather than tools to promote daily exercise as they were intentionally designed for. In addition, the stress levels of many people in our society are at an all-time high. And unfortunately, sickness that leads to death has become an acceptable concept in most people's minds.

The Total Package

For example, some people when diagnosed with a sickness that if unchecked could lead to death, tend to accommodate the sickness rather than believing for the sickness to be healed. What I mean by accommodating the sickness is that they begin to immediately adjust their lifestyles to "make room" for the sickness. They begin to act and do things as if they have had the sickness for years. Although they could totally refute the possibility of being sick at all, they deliberately choose not to. After all, doctors can make mistakes; it's called human error. However, many choose to accept in their minds that sickness is just an inevitable reality of life. This madness has become such a common way of thinking within society that thinking otherwise or "thinking healthy" is considered abnormal.

During the limited occasions that I view television it amazes me when I watch commercials about new drug products that are advertised to the general public.

Just the other day, one commercial advertised a drug that claimed to relieve pain in the muscles, mainly due to arthritis. The pharmaceutical company promised that their product would alleviate all pain and discomfort associated with arthritis. However, before the commercial ended, it gave a listing (a type of legal disclosure) of all the potential side effects.

Some of these side effects included aneurysm; sudden heart failure; weakened eyesight, possible blindness; internal bleeding; chronic bleeding; vomiting; and unexplained weight loss. At the end of the commercial they were kind enough to inform you not to use this medication unless you first consulted with your doctor. Considering the list of possible side effects, if you were to use this wonder drug you'd probably wind up needing a mortician, not a doctor.

While the drug industry does not unfairly withhold information from the general public concerning possible side effects, millions of people still choose to drug themselves rather than seek out newer and alternate methods of healing. I call this behavior "typical insanity." The good news is that there is hope for the sickened soul. However, that hope is only accessed when you recognize the need to search out possibilities in health and healing that maybe you have never explored before.

> *Ask, and it will be given to you; seek, and you will find; knock, and it will be opened to you. For everyone who asks receives, and he who seeks finds, and to him who knocks it will be opened* (Matthew 7:7-8).

The second unfortunate truth is that most people will die broke, leaving their family members to bear the unwanted burden of paying the funeral expenses. As hard as that truth is to digest, it still remains true. In the same way that people in society have become satisfied with sickness many also have become accustomed to living life from paycheck to paycheck. They too have become comfortable paying interest rates as high as 24.9 percent on their credit cards, driving them deeper into a spiral of debt.

Some people ask me for advice about their retirement and then I find out that their primary house is not paid off and they still have a car payment. Those expenses can add up to more than 50 percent of their pension or retirement income, so after tax they are still struggling to make ends meet. Retirement should be about having fun and choices, not struggle and worry.

We realize that traps are laid everywhere to lure you into debt. Offers are made available through the mail, at your local grocery and department stores, gas stations, and even in the student union centers at most colleges and universities. Before average high school students have completed twelfth grade, they have had enormous opportunities to get credit cards in their names, regardless of whether they have a job or not.

The Total Package

If you own a computer and use email you are probably inundated with messages claiming to get you out of debt by getting you into more debt by applying for their loans. I fully realize that the temptation is great to sign your name or in other words, "sign your life away." That may sound a little extreme, but for all intent and purposes you must begin to see it just that way, as exchanging the precious moments of your life for things that serve little or no purpose to you once you have purchased them.

Perhaps you have heard people make misinformed statements such as, "I'm broke"; "I'll *never* be able to afford that"; or "I just don't have enough money to make ends meet." Although most people don't realize it, statements like these have literally created not only a negative thought pattern which you govern yourself by, but also have created your material and spiritual world. What you say long enough will become a part of your daily actions, then an embedded part of your belief system. Once you begin to believe what you say, you will become what you believe—whether good or bad.

In my opinion I believe that the most ridiculous statement I have ever heard anyone say concerning money is this: "Money is not important." I am immediately taken back several steps by the gross ignorance and denial that are connected to making such an empty statement. Everything in this material world that we live in is directly connected to money. Notice, I did not say everything in the spiritual world; I said *the material world*. And believe it or not, you live in this material world.

When a person positions their lips to utter such foolishness as "Money is not important," I know immediately that they suffer with great financial problems. Only the poor in finances and the poor in knowledge could ever utter such a gross misconception. And yet, this is the prevailing mindset of the majority of people within our society.

Introduction

A feast is made for laughter, and wine makes merry; but money answers everything (Ecclesiastes 10:19).

Money is important, very important. You will only attract it when you realize its importance. Those who are rich understand the importance of money and because of that they attract it. That which you devalue or think is not important you will never have. Or if by chance you acquire it, you won't keep it for long, just as divorces occur when either one or both people in the bonds of marriage believe that their spouse is not as important as they were when they married them.

You will lose your job when it becomes unimportant to you. You will show up late, leave early, and take long lunch breaks—then finally get fired. Your relationship with God will begin to decline when you place everything else as a higher priority than loving Him. It's no different with money. If money is not important to you, you will always struggle to make ends meet. In all reality the reason why so many people devalue money is because they are afraid of two things. First, many people are afraid of doing the things that cause money to multiply, such as owning a business and investing. They are afraid of the risk involved in both ventures—so afraid that they choose to do nothing instead. They bury their money in the sand and live life wondering why they can't have more. Second, many people are afraid that acquiring material wealth will cause them to become evil and unkind people.

Many have been falsely indoctrinated into believing that those with little or no money at all have a greater chance at living a "holy" and consecrated life before God. Fortunately for the devil, millions of Christians have bought into this scandalous lie that has shrouded the Body of Christ with poverty in epic proportions. Although I am usually bothered by generalizations, I can safely say that from my travels I have noticed that most church folk are broke.

The Total Package

To add to that, most pastors have a difficult time raising the funds needed to meet their weekly expenses, let alone their annual budgets. Whereas in times past the "small church" was the one with the greater financial struggles, the mega-churches have within the past two decades joined their ranks. Many mega-churches miserably struggle each month to feed the monster of ministry, television expense, and lofty mortgage payments. The cure—better management and more money.

What about those college expenses that are still unpaid? Let's be honest. Can you comfortably live your life free of financial worry right now? If you cannot, this book was written for you whether your manifested income is $20,000 or $200,000. This book was written as a testament of hope—hope for healing and hope for wealth. This work is not about avarice and greed. It is not about being healthy so that you can run off and pursue mundane pursuits. It's about believing that you can in this lifetime have the total package—health and wealth.

So what exactly should you expect from this book? You can expect a blueprint that will show you how to live the lifestyle of the healed and whole. Is it better to pay a doctor thousands of dollars to treat a disease or is it better to avoid contracting the disease altogether? This book is about prevention.

We give you a guide that shows you how to avoid the debt traps that are so prevalent within society and guide you back to a healthy way of life. If you change the way you think, you will change the world—and the world can be changed one person at a time. We intend to change the way you think about health and wealth forever. However, we can only do it with your help. Make the change. Turn the page.

Listen, I tell you a mystery: We will not all sleep, but we will all be changed (1 Corinthians 15:51 NIV).

Part 1

The Diagnosis

"A careful examination and analysis of the facts in an attempt to understand or explain something."

The Total Package

Chapter One

You Perish for the Lack of Knowledge

My people are destroyed for lack of knowledge. Because you have rejected knowledge, I also will reject you from being priest for Me; because you have forgotten the law of your God, I also will forget your children (Hosea 4:6).

If you suffer destruction in your health or personal finances, in your business, spiritual life, or relationships, the principle reason can be easily tied to your lack of knowledge. Believe it or not, it is the areas you are most ignorant of that will eventually destroy you. There is no wonder why much of the biblical Proverbs continuously reminds us of the importance of seeking knowledge. And although we live in the most technologically advanced information age ever, people still choose to live sick and broke.

Notice that I said *choose*. One of the first things you need to learn is that walking in divine health and obtaining financial abundance are choices. They don't happen by accident. Next you must know that walking in divine health and gaining financial abundance are journeys that eventually become lifestyles, not just something you do every now and then. As natural as it is for a bird to fly in the skies and as effortless as fish swim in the ocean, so shall your health and wealth become to you once you have acquired the right kind of knowledge.

"Walking in divine health and obtaining financial abundance are choices."

My words may sound like a wise proverb...that's because they are a wise proverb—duh? I am trying to take the pain out of life, the pain associated with desperately struggling to stay alive. That will only happen when you come to the knowledge that there are some things you are not doing correctly that need to be changed in your life. I recognize that there are some things you are presently doing that are working for you. By all means, keep doing those things.

However, I hope to enlighten you to things that you are unaware of that could be making your financial and health life miserable and unfruitful. Based on the enormous amount of information you will be given, I want you to begin making daily steps, baby steps toward the goal you have envisioned. You don't have to run like a sprinter and try to accomplish everything in one day, one week, or even a month's time.

If you gradually move forward, making constant progress, in time you will begin to see unbelievable improvement. Again, don't feel the need to rush the process. The goal is for you to accept good health and increase wealth as a lifestyle, not the latest fad. So embrace this opportunity to explore and learn something that you may not have known before.

The Forbidden "C" Word

When I was growing up, cancer was a forbidden topic of discussion among most members of my family. I can clearly remember overhearing a conversation as a child about a relative, an aunt or uncle, who was diagnosed with cancer. The announcement alone immediately brought a feeling of despair and a sense of hopelessness into the room. It seemed as if the very thought of someone getting cancer represented the beginning of the end of their life. Because they were sure that death was imminent, all the family members showed their concern and sympathy for the person diagnosed with cancer.

Unfortunately, no one ever seemed to offer my relatives any hope simply because they did not *know* that any such hope existed. Worse yet was the fact that we were forbidden to talk freely or ask questions about our uncle or aunt's sickness. We could never mention the word *cancer* because it had become the forbidden "C" word. My other siblings would be spanked or at least strictly reprimanded for ever using the word.

Since we were forewarned of this, we wisely refrained from using the word altogether. Interestingly, I happened to be born at the end of June. This meant that my zodiac sign was cancer, symbolized by the crab. In our household we did not believe in all the hype about signs of the constellation anyway, so I choose not to mention the word even if it was related to my birth sign.

Both my grandmother and grandfather had died from this debilitating disease. Still, I could not freely discuss his or her sickness with anyone. I am sure that one of the reasons I was not allowed to discuss this topic with liberty is because of the pain that is commonly associated with the loss of a beloved one. The thought of cancer brought back many painful memories of how much their loved one suffered with this disease. That, I could understand. However, the other reason no one wanted to talk freely on the subject is because, like old family secrets, it became a taboo topic.

Most people have come to accept the disease of cancer as a mysterious illness with little chance of being cured. Because of this belief, most people would rather not talk about it. But the idea that cancer is incurable is simply not true. The real problem is that there are not enough people freely dialoging about this subject to bring about a level of comfort when the topic strikes up. Do you believe that the average person would start becoming aloof, reclusive, and afraid if they found out that their mother or father was diagnosed with the influenza virus, commonly known as the flu? Probably not.

We have for the most part access to medicines and conventional herbs that guard against and in many cases prevent getting the flu altogether. Although the United States Center for Disease Control and Prevention (CDC) estimates that nearly 20,000 people die each year from the flu, most Americans feel pretty confident that the flu won't kill them. But did you know that the influenza pandemic that occurred between 1918 and 1919—the worst on record—killed about 500,000 people in the United States and more than 20 million people worldwide?

If these figures represented our present-day reality, the flu would tie with cancer as being the second leading killer in America. Coupled with pneumonia, influenza still ranks as the seventh leading cause of death in the United States. The point is that most people feel as if we have a reasonable handle on this disease so it no longer scares them as it did back in 1918.

What caused the panic to go away even though the virus is still alive and kills people? Why are most people not paranoid about getting the flu and dying from it? Successful research and study of how to control and prevent this virus are the main reasons why we feel more secure. I want to reiterate the fact that people are still dying from this disease. However, since we now have more *knowledge* on the subject, we don't worry as much anymore. In this instance knowledge really has armed us with power. It has the power to alleviate our worries.

You probably did not *know* that nearly 100,000 people die each year from accidents, which includes work-related accidents

6

and automobile accidents. Although thousands of people die annually from car crashes, most people are not afraid to get in or even drive a car. Most people do not consider the risk of death nor are they afraid to operate the same type of vehicle that caused death for others.

The reason they are so confident is because they have *knowledge*. They choose to obey the rules of the road. Smart people won't drink and drive. Most responsible drivers will pull over to the side of the road if they need to talk on their cellular phone, especially if it is a long and involved conversation. Truck drivers are told to get proper sleep before going on long trips and take breaks during extended runs. These are just a few of the many things that you can do to help lessen the fear associated with automobile death.

Because you know these things, you have no problem acting on what you know. But when considering cancer, many people still do not know how to live a lifestyle that will help lessen the chances of getting cancer altogether. It is what they do not know that will inevitably kill them, not the disease alone. The disease can't kill you if you know the cure, or better yet, know how to prevent it.

Part of the diagnosis concerning your present state of health is that you lack knowledge. As already stated, lack of knowledge will kill you, but ignoring knowledge will kill you even faster. Consider that smoking kills more than one million people each year in the Americas, yet cigarette sales continue to soar, even in states that impose a high tax on the sale of cigarettes.

No one has to diligently search for information as to whether or not cigarette smoking can hinder good health. Clearly marked in bold large print on every cigarette pack, the Surgeon General has declared that smoking is hazardous to your health and may cause cancer. Other statements warn pregnant women and nursing mothers of the negative effect that smoking may have on their child. Yet even with these warnings people still ignore the truth.

And it always freaks me out when smokers get cancer or lung failure and act as if they are surprised. The logic is very simple. Oxygen is the number-one, most primary nutrient to every cell in your body. Although Jesus fasted for 40 days without any food and the human body can do without water for a few days, you can only go for minutes, really seconds, without air and oxygen. After that your brain dies, and you are dead.

When you smoke, you are willfully and knowingly destroying the only organ in your body that digests and assimilates oxygen. If your lungs fail, no other organ can take their place. Every time you smoke, you are clogging the pores on the surface of your lungs with tar, slowly killing yourself. Smoking is a type of assisted suicide. If you smoke you cannot be healthy.

Believe me, I am not trying to preach to you; I am only trying to influence you to change your way of thinking. It's the choices that you make on a day-to-day basis that determine what you have right now and who you are. And if you continually ignore knowledge, you will be destroyed. Have you ever heard people say things like, "I don't care what you say; I am going to do it the way I've always done it; I have never heard anything like that in all my life; all this new-age modern stuff is foolishness"?

If you have heard statements like these, you have come face-to-face with a fool, a person who will die because of his or her own ignorance. People with such a limited view on life will never be helped because they don't want help. They will always live in constant fear that some dreadful disease will someday overtake them. What a horrible way to live life.

Personally, I don't fear cancer, because I have knowledge. I *know* some foods to avoid that will increase my risk of cancer. I also know what foods and supplements to include in my eating plan to help fight cancer. I know what things to do and what not to do to help me decrease the possibility of ever getting cancer. And I'm aware of those places that I should never expose myself to if I don't want to get cancer. Because I have all this knowledge I don't worry about cancer. It's not hard for me to live this way.

You know not to jam a piece of metal into an electrical socket. Hopefully you fully understand the immediate consequences for doing something so stupid. It's not hard for you to refrain from doing something so ridiculous...you just don't. It's the same way with any lifestyle habits once you make it a priority to live healthy.

My Mother's Cancer Battle

In the event that one of your relatives, perhaps your father or mother, is diagnosed with cancer, would you be able to take off one week every month to tend to their physical needs until they regained health? Within the past couple years I have found myself in this unfortunate situation.

More than ever I now understand that cancer is not only a disease that takes over the whole body, but actually takes over the whole family. When we discovered my mother had lung cancer, I was shocked and saddened at the same time. My father had already battled prostate cancer just one year before.

Thank God, he was successfully treated and now once again leads the productive life that he had previously led. I thought I was finished dealing with the cancer situation in my family after my father's bout. However, during the Christmas holiday, I suspected that something was seriously wrong when I noticed that my mom was getting unusually thin. By the time doctors diagnosed her, the cancer had already spread to three areas of her body.

My brother and sister met and made the determination that our mother could not continue to work her job in the school system in WestPoint, Mississippi. In time her condition worsened. Her ability to move her legs ceased. We made the decision to move her back to Minnesota. To this day we still maintain her home in Mississippi because we want her to always know she has a place to come back to when she fully recovers.

I am thankful that God has afforded me the privilege to be able to take a week off each month without having any financial worries or facing financial depravity. I realize that most people are not in a position to be able to do this. My goal is to help other people gain the resources so that they can also stay with their loved ones in times of desperate need without having to worry about their money situation.

Health can bring wealth; but wealth, when it stands alone, has its limitations. Wealth can buy the best doctors and the finest medications in the world; however, all my money or even all the money in the world cannot immediately cure my mother's condition. I know that a divine intervention from God is what she needs. I live every day of my life expecting just that.

If your relative suddenly became sick, consider the following financial questions that you might have to face:

1. What is your parent's income if they could not work today? How much would they receive from social security, their pension plan, 401K, 403B, or other retirement accounts and income from rental property?

2. Weigh their income against their present debts. Do they have a balance on their home mortgage? What is the balance on their credit cards and other monthly debts?

3. What is the total amount of their ongoing monthly expenses, such as natural gas, electric, and telephone bills? Don't forget to calculate food expenses.

4. Do they have a long-term care policy or some other income replacement vehicle?

After you have added all the expenses and weighed them against the income, you should determine whether there is a gap between the income and outflow. If there is a gap, you must close it quickly. In other words, you must come up with the amount of money needed to cover your loved one's expenses, taking into account long-term care and developing a savings or debt reduction plan.

Let me share a sample of some of the (non-medical) costs involved in caring for my mother:

1. My monthly roundtrip airfare is anywhere from $250 to $500 traveling from Los Angeles to Mississippi or Minnesota.

2. My rental car usually costs from $200 to $400. I tend to rent a full-size car or bigger because everyone in my family is quite tall. I'm 6'4". Also, because my mother drove a Cadillac in Mississippi, we drive the same car. I want to make her feel as comfortable as we can.

3. Mom's groceries and personal items total about $300 each month. (Note that these figures do not include her mortgage or utilities for her home in Mississippi.)

When I was about 19 I attended a personal finance class. I remember my instructor giving an oral assignment to everyone instructing us to tell the class what our short, medium, and long-range goals were. When it was my turn, I stood up and told everyone I didn't have to make a long-range goal because I was going to retire by the time I was 35.

Because of His goodness, God decided that I would go into semi-retirement at age 33. I visit my mother for one week out of every month. That totals to more than three months off work per year. (Also each month, I facilitate seminars at churches around the United States and the Caribbean.) When one of my mother's lungs collapsed, I made the decision that she doesn't have to battle cancer alone. Her sickness not only became my concern but also my responsibility.

The Total Package

Because I have financial freedom, I go to treatment with Mother every month. One of my coworkers asked me, "George, how can you take so much time off? Is it okay with your boss?" I informed her that Jesus is my first boss and so spending time with my mother in her time of great need is not optional; my job is.

I can always get another job; I cannot get another mother and may not have another opportunity to spend more time with her. I don't regret any time I spend with her. I am so thankful to God that I planted financial seeds more than ten years ago and because of that I now have the means to take good care of her. I have developed multiple streams of income. I hope to plant that same seed in your spirit today. If God did it for me, Healso can do it for you.

Invest Is Not a Four-Letter Word

I realize that it may take a little time for most folk to talk comfortably about cancer, particularly if you have lost a friend or relative to this disease. That I can understand. What I can't understand is how anyone in the world expects to grow rich or at least be financially comfortable if they continue to avoid the word *invest*.

We all are aware of some four-letter words in American culture that we consciously avoid using because they are totally vulgar and most offensive. But perhaps you may not have known this: I-N-V-E-S-T is not a four-letter word. It is not vulgar, and neither should it offend the one using it or the one who hears it.

The truth is that you will never be wealthy until you begin investing. Part of your financial diagnosis suggests that you are dying financially because you won't invest. Usually people don't invest because they either don't have the money available to them or they don't know how to invest. Don't worry, as you read on, I will help you to better understand the whole investment process.

There are some things you have to understand about money before you will ever be a financial success. The first thing is that

12

you will never become financially independent simply by working a job. J.O.B. is an acronym for Just Over Broke. That is what most people are who are tied to their job. Your job will never give you enough money to become financially free. It will only give you enough money to last one week.

"*Your job will never give you enough money to become financially free. It will only give you enough money to last one week.*"

That is exactly why you have to go back to work every Monday whether you want to or not. You only get one week's worth of money and no one can live comfortably that way. On top of that, your job may be here today and gone tomorrow. With corporate downsizing and layoffs you are never sure that your job is secure from one day to another. Nothing except God and His Word are for sure. They are the only things you can count on.

The grass withers and the flowers fall, but the word of our God stands forever (Isaiah 40:8 NIV).

Our federal government has recently frozen all spending and hiring in federally funded organizations in order to acquire more money to fight against terrorism within our country and abroad and to pay for the high expense of war. Even after the war has ended someone will still have to pay the bills. Take a wild guess who's going to pay.

You've guessed correctly. You are. You ask, "How will I pay?" You will pay monetarily in several ways. Let me list a few for your knowledge's sake. The easiest, quickest, and most obvious way to raise revenue is to increase your taxes. The taxes that most people pay over their lifetime is the single largest bill they will ever have.

You will pay more in taxes than you will for your home, your yacht, or your child's education. Unfortunately, most people will give more to the federal government in taxes than they ever will to God since He requires less finances from you than the government does. What can you do about this? Well, you can write your congressman. However, by the time he properly deals with your concern, a whole new administration will have begun. So scratch that thought.

The better choice is to hire the best tax strategist you can afford. I did not say tax service or accountant. There is a clear difference between a person who is good with numbers and figures and a person who seeks every possible way to save you money. You need a person who works strategies—legal strategies to find breaks that will help you pay the least amount in taxes. That will put you on the road to increase.

So you realize that you are going to be taxed to death. There are some other truths that you are going to have to face. Realize too that your 401K will change to a 301K to a 201K to a 101K eventually to a lowercase k. I'm not criticizing 401K's; they have been a wonderful choice to invest in. What I am trying to convey is that if you are putting all your eggs in your 401K you may need to think about other strategies to invest your money into. I trust that you realize that if you are my age (thirty-some years old), you may never see any social security money when you retire. I really hate to be the one to tell you this, but your social security money has been spent, long ago.

So you are going to have to learn other ways to invest to get ahead. Financially speaking you have a bad case of the flu and until you start taking the medication prescribed, you will remain sick. You may not like to or want to, but you must start investing in things that will yield better dividends rather than in what you are already investing.

You Are Always Investing, Even Though You May Not Know It

The recent scandals within the Enron Corporation and the MCI WorldCom Corporation totally shocked our nation. Most people could

14

not believe just how dishonest and evil corporate leaders could actually be. In short, the Enron Corporation allegedly created more than nine billion dollars in assets out of thin air. In other words, they created their wealth on paper, but not in reality.

They persuaded people to invest in their company based on written imaginary figures. When the truth was discovered that the company was not worth what they had claimed to be, thousands of investors lost all their investment money, leaving some people totally broke and others violently angry. Most investors who were associated with Enron felt jaded and taken advantage of. A similar situation happened with MCI WorldCom causing its investors to lose money also.

After these unfortunate situations happened, I noticed that many people, who although they did not have their money invested in either Enron or MCI WorldCom, became suspicious of other companies. Some people started cashing in their stocks, bonds, and mutual funds prematurely in an effort to safeguard themselves from what they thought was imminent doom. Their fearful actions sent a negative message throughout the entire country, "Don't invest, you'll lose." Although these two scenarios are isolated incidences and do not represent the strong character of more than thirty thousand other companies, people still choose to be afraid.

For God has not given us a spirit of fear, but of power and of love and of a sound mind (2 Timothy 1:7).

Let me point out that the people who were the most fearful and stopped investing altogether were people who did not have *knowledge* about investing. Knowledgeable people understand that when one investment does not work, they must feverishly seek out one that will. Why? Investors have to keep investing. It's the nature of the beast. Once you stop investing, life stops. It's as simple as that. The point is that everybody is an investor. You regularly invest in something

15

whether you know it or not. You are either investing into yourself or investing into someone else's empire.

If you work, you get paid. If you are not getting paid for work, then you are either a volunteer or a slave. (And if you are a slave, please write your congressman letting him know, since slavery has been illegal for more than one hundred years.) When you get paid, you can do one of three things with your money: spend it, lend it, which is what you do when you put your money in the bank, or own something. You can have two people who earn the same income, live in the same neighborhood, have relatively an equal share of expenses, and have the same amount of children to care for; yet, they each show a very different financial situation.

One person invests money out of every paycheck into one or more of his investment portfolios that include but are not limited to stocks and bonds, income-producing real estate, and a solid and proven network marketing business. He budgets a certain amount of money each week that gets deposited into a fund specifically for those purposes. He takes great pleasure in knowing that as time goes on, his investments will continue to increase. Knowing that gives him a sense of security because his family will not have to worry about financial lack even in the worst of times.

The other person does not believe that he has enough money to invest. He is the guy who is broke and always trying to talk his friend out of investing. He'll say, "You know you're going to lose all your money. You're just trying to be like those rich folks." Because of his lack of knowledge, he mistakenly thinks that only the rich have the kind of money to invest in anything really worthwhile. Later the broke guy will need to borrow money from the investor. But that may not be a good investment.

So he chooses to *invest* in his alcohol addiction and cigarette-smoking obsession. He religiously invests the very same amount of money each week into his compulsive habits. Like clockwork, when Friday comes he cashes his check at the bank and immediately makes his deposit at his favorite spirit shop. As time continues, his children graduate from high school and desire to go on to college.

Sadly, he does not have even enough money to purchase a gift for his first graduating senior. It is obvious that his child's future is bleak since her drunken father has chosen to invest more than 20 years into his habits rather than investing in something that would have yielded him a profit. He eventually loses his home, then his job. Now he is homeless wandering from shelter to shelter. The only thing important to him is where and when he will get his next drink.

"More money will not solve your problems."

Everyone is always investing in something. Consider how much money the cigarette store made over the 20 years of investing this man's money for him. Surely, their investment has paid off favorably using his money. Imagine just how many businesses have invested into something for their benefit with the money you have freely given to them over the years. Had you done what they did with your money, you'd be rich now.

What happened in the Enron scandal was horrible. However, the truth remains that life goes on. Hopefully, we all can learn lessons from their failures. Avarice and greed are very much alive in our society. Because of that, people influenced by the devil will at times do anything to get money. Some will lie, cheat, steal, and in some cases even murder innocent people.

So don't listen to anyone who tells you anything other than the law of investing will always work for the person who works it. Incidentally, this law of investing is a financial term that has its roots in spiritual law. In the spiritual world we call this the law of sowing and reaping. No matter what happens, no matter how bad times appear to be, the law of sowing and reaping, the law of investing, will never cease.

For whatever a man sows, that he will also reap (Galatians 6:7).

The Total Package

I Don't Make Enough Money

Many people believe they have financial troubles because they don't have enough money. I know that it sounds like a good excuse. It may even garner some sympathy for you. But the truth is, more money will not solve your problems. You can get financially ahead with what you have right now.

It's your thinking that produces your habits and it's those habits that produce your reality. So in order to change your present situation, you have to begin by changing the way you think. More money will only create more of what you are doing right now. Money is a magnifier. Money will only enlarge what and who you are. If you are an alcoholic, more money will increase your spending on more alcohol. In some cases you might even begin to purchase very expensive wines.

More money increases your spending habits. If you love cars, more money will allow you to purchase more expensive cars with higher maintenance costs. If you love to eat, more money will translate you from your favorite all-you-can-eat buffet to the world's finest five-star gourmet restaurants. This list can go on and on. The issue is that if you don't change your ways, you will remain financially distressed, no matter how much money you have.

The solution for financial success is income (money) combined with less outgo (disciplined spending). The formula sounds simple yet it seems so hard to get most people to follow. It amounts to self-control over your emotions because that is the primary motivating factor that causes most people to spend in the first place. Subsequently, literally billions of dollars are spent annually on advertising.

Advertisers know so well that if they can get you to watch their commercials, read their magazine ads, or spot a billboard, they can get you to buy a product. They can even get you to buy a product that you are not interested in. It works. And until you finish reading this book, most advertisers have more knowledge than you about how your emotions and mind work.

18

You Hold a Master's Degree in Spending Money

We all can learn more in subjects concerning money. However, the one financial course that most people have mastered, whether they are poor or rich, is the area of spending. You know how to spend. Every time you get money, part if not all of it goes toward a purchase that you were waiting for. This law of spending can properly be labeled as the law of exchange.

You give the seller your money in exchange for something that you believe is of equal or greater value than your money. That something could be a piece of clothing, a car, a home, a DVD player, jewelry, food, a dream vacation or this book. The issue is that most things you purchase depreciate in monetary value the moment your purchase is made.

The key is not to stop spending altogether. That would not be realistic. Your goal is to begin to spend more on things that have the propensity to make you money, things that will create wealth. Once you learn and understand what to buy from what not to buy you will have matriculated into the Ph.D. program in spending. That's the part that the rich understand and the poor do not. You must know when to spend and what to spend on. Those two factors are the most crucial things to know about the law of spending.

So before you spend, first ask yourself the question, "Is what I am about to purchase going to yield an even or greater exchange value than it costs for the product or item?" That may sound a bit far-fetched, but believe me, it's worth it. That is what differentiates the "haves" from the "have-nots."

If you don't need it nor were you in the market for it, then don't purchase it. Don't be emotionally driven by big sales or advertisers trying to get you to purchase what you have never dreamed of having. Walk past the sales; it's not your time yet. You have bigger and better dreams than merely buying another this or that. You are on your way from mastering spending to being able to teach others how to properly spend.

The Total Package

No More Excuses

Let's make a pact right now. From this day forth you will commit to seeking knowledge. If that means that you have to read more than you ever have, go to seminars, or listen to teaching tapes, then do it. We are committed to assisting you in your fight for financial and physical liberty. But we can't do it without your help.

Right now, renounce all of Satan's lies. Do not accept nor make any more excuses for your present condition. Whether you have been sick for a prolonged time or financially broke since birth, do not accept this condition as your permanent lifestyle. God's Word promises that you can have more than you are experiencing right now.

Let's do an exercise. I have created a list of some of the most common excuses concerning lack of healthy living and financial freedom. The Word of God is powerful, so powerful that it can change your bleak situation into a blossoming reality. So for every excuse that I list, there is a corresponding Scripture to refute that excuse. Knowing what God says about your health and wealth far outweighs the opinion of any man. So let's begin.

"My family has always had a certain sickness or disease, so I know that I am at high risk for the same thing. It is sort of a genetic curse in my bloodline."

"As far back as I can remember my family has always been poor. I grew up very poor. I guess I just inherited a curse of poverty."

God's Word says:

Christ has redeemed us from the curse of the law, having become a curse for us (for it is written, "Cursed is everyone who hangs on a tree"), that the blessing of Abraham might come upon the Gentiles in Christ Jesus, that we might receive the promise of the Spirit through faith (Galatians 3:13-14).

"No matter what I do I just can't seem to get ahead financially. It seems like the rich folk have all the money and all the power. It's just not fair."

God's Word says:

And you shall remember the Lord your God, for it is He who gives you power to get wealth, that He may establish His covenant which He swore to your fathers, as it is this day (Deuteronomy 8:18).

"I really don't want to live in abundance. I just want to have enough to get by in life. I really don't need all that much."

God's Word says:

The thief does not come except to steal, and to kill, and to destroy. I have come that they may have life, and that they may have it more abundantly (John 10:10).

"Maybe it's just God's will for me to be sick. Perhaps God has willed for me to die."

God's Word says:

Beloved, I pray that you may prosper in all things and be in health, just as your soul prospers (3 John 2).

"I think it's difficult for someone to love God and be wealthy. You have to choose one or the other. Don't you?"

God's Word says:

Abram was very rich in livestock, in silver, and in gold (Genesis 13:2).

The Total Package

This day I call heaven and earth as witnesses against you that I have set before you life and death, blessings and curses. Now choose life, so that you and your children may live and that you may love the Lord your God, listen to His voice, and hold fast to Him. For the Lord is your life, and He will give you many years in the land He swore to give to your fathers, Abraham, Isaac and Jacob (Deuteronomy 30:19-20 NIV).

"I've carried this sickness so long I don't know if I will ever get better. Most of the time, I feel as if I am all alone in my struggle."

God's Word says:

Surely He has borne our griefs and carried our sorrows; yet we esteemed Him stricken, smitten by God, and afflicted. But He was wounded for our transgressions, He was bruised for our iniquities; the chastisement for our peace was upon Him, and by His stripes we are healed (Isaiah 53:4-5).

Chapter Two

A Nation Enslaved

Before we get into the mechanics, the nuts and bolts of finances, if you will, it is necessary for us to conduct a thorough examination of the problem of financial depravity in our society. This is pertinent to the whole diagnostic process. If we can understand how we got into this situation in the first place, we may have a better chance of redeeming ourselves from the curse of poverty.

Some of you may have just cringed at the thought of me labeling poverty as a curse. I get it all the time. People say, "You can't call poverty a curse. That's wrong. There's a whole lot of good people who are just outright poor, and they can't help it." Notice I did not say that the people themselves were a curse. I said that they inherited or in some cases legally adopted poverty as their personal companion, which is a curse no matter which way you slice it.

I like to define poverty as being destitute of earthly goods that have become of widespread importance in our modern-day society. For example, most people would probably agree that a car has become a needed earthly good in our society, although you could ride around town in a horse and buggy like they did one hundred years ago. And I am certain that given the right amount of time, you would be able to get to your destination. It may not be as comfortable as other methods of transportation, but it would do.

The only problem is that you cannot drive a horse and buggy on any highway in the United States of America because it's illegal. That simply means that you are going to be forced to accepting a newer more efficient means of travel, particularly if you need to travel from Connecticut to California. For most people a more affordable choice than a Gulf Stream 3 jet would probably be a car.

Although you don't have to own a Rolls Royce Corniche Convertible, it would probably make sense for you to purchase the most quality vehicle that your money can buy. The point is that a car is necessary. More important than owning a car, is to own shelter, commonly referred to as a house.

The poor mindset would argue that it is not necessary for a person to own a home. After all, you could live outdoors, especially if you live in sunny San Diego, California. You could live in the mountains and eat wild locust and honey. Some theologians could justify that since John the Baptist lived a sacrificial lifestyle, every Christian believer should also adopt a meager way to live.

But if you will be honest, you will have to admit that owning a home is more than just the American dream; it's a necessity. If it is not a necessity for you, then make it one. You might say, "Well, I can always rent; I don't have to own." That train of thought is one of the main reasons why people remain broke. Renting will always make your landlord richer and you "broker." You must understand that getting wealthy is all about owning, not borrowing or renting. Realize this financial truth: If you are renting, your rent will *always* increase. And as you continue to live, the rate of inflation will eventually eat you alive. You've got to think *ownership*.

Change your thinking. Stop making excuses for why you aren't prosperous. As we have already covered, your prosperity is directly connected to what you know. The formula is: No knowledge— no prosperity. Prosperity is a friend of the person who will take time to understand the "how to" of money, investing and creating wealth out of nothing. But you must first accept that prosperity is a state of mind.

Beloved, I pray that you may prosper in all things and be in health, just as your soul prospers (3 John 2).

Isn't it interesting that this Scripture informs us that both health and financial prosperity will be in direct correlation to how your soul, or in other words, the human mind prospers. If your mind is not prospering in the Word concerning wealth and health, then you will not benefit from those areas. If you are literally researching, meditating, and digesting every word concerning healing and wealth throughout the Bible, then you will become very well to do. The reason I am so convinced that the Word of God works is because I am living proof of it.

Stop saying things like, "I can wear anything; it doesn't make any difference what I put on. All you need is just one pair of shoes; you've only got one pair of feet. I can eat anything; it doesn't matter to me. This house is just too big; you can only live in one room at a time anyway. My four hundred-dollar car works just as good as your Mercedes Benz; they'll both get you from point A to point B."

You know as well as I do that this list of poverty-filled statements could continue on forever. Usually when you hear people say something like this, they are trying their best to hide the reality within. They, like most people, would love to enjoy the best that life has to offer; but they have become a victim of their surroundings. They have become an enslaved people—a people who reverberate the words that their master commands them to speak. For many, these words have become a doctrine or creed and a tainted testament to live by. For them, depravity and indebtedness have become a state of mind.

Slavery Is a State of Mind

For as he thinketh in his heart, so is he (Proverbs 23:7 KJV).

Slavery for anyone who has been enslaved is always an extremely sensitive topic, and rightfully so. It is unfair to expect Jews to ever cease from reminding their people and the world of the diabolical acts the Nazis perpetrated against their people, exterminating more than six million European Jews prior to World War II. Often, we are cautioned to forget things and put them behind us. However, some things we simply cannot forget. To forget such things would set the stage for history to repeat itself. Most people who have suffered tragedy would not want to perpetuate the cycle. For most, it would be far too painful. Consider that the whole concept of Christianity is based on the believer *remembering* what Jesus Christ went through in order to redeem us back to the Father.

Our Lord suffered horrific negative treatment. Jesus was the victim of lies, scandal, and unprecedented abuse. I am certain that He forgave His enemies. However, if we forget what He did on our behalf, it would not only be ridiculous but would also invalidate the whole foundation of the Christian faith.

Black people in America are often reminded of the physical cruelties inflicted on their ancestors by their evil slave masters. They were separated from their families; children were taken from their mothers at birth never to see them again. Working long hours without compensation had become a normal way of living. They did not expect to receive compensation. They were robbed of their heritage, their history, and for many their destinies. However, more tragic than

26

the actual atrocities inflicted upon the slaves was the permanent damage it caused to their thinking.

Although the phrase "slave mentality" has been used in a loose way, its meaning reaches further than most people actually realize. Slave mentality is a way of thinking. It is a mindset that does not expect to receive anything valuable in life. It views the oppressor as a friend, and it looks at the one called to deliver them as a demagogue.

For our purpose in this section, the words *slavery* and *debt* will be used interchangeably. I believe these words can be easily swapped because, for the most part, they have the same meaning. I know for sure that they both produce the same outcome—bondage and servitude to systems.

For example, most people would never challenge the authority or accuracy of the Internal Revenue Service on income tax matters. However, the people who work there are human just like you and me. They too are prone to make mistakes and are subject to failure. Yet most people take their word for everything whirled at them. Why? The Internal Revenue Service represents a system and slaves are trained well not to challenge systems.

The Department of Children and Families are neither the FBI nor the CIA yet most people are afraid to biblically correct and punish their children for doing wrong, fearing that the DCF will take their children away from them. Slaves are afraid to challenge systems. They are afraid to go against the status quo. People who suffer with this mindset never ask questions that may lead to their freedom, but instead accept life the way it is rather than how it should be.

This is exactly why people are drowning in debt today. Most people have accepted debt as a common or normal lifestyle. Just try announcing to your family and friends that you've received some wonderful new information concerning financial freedom and you are going to be debt free. I'm sure you will be disappointed by their response: "You know that doesn't make any sense. It's impossible for you to be debt free. You have got to have some debt. Debt is normal. You must be listening to some cultic teachings or something."

Most people cannot visualize themselves as being debt free because possessing unusual amounts of debt has become an accept-able way of living for most people. Just like most people expect to catch a cold or get a headache at some time throughout the year, they also expect to get in debt and stay there. The reason why it seems so normal is because your average person carries far more debt than they can afford to pay, even in a lifetime.

Consider these statistics from www.CardWeb.com:[1]

- *The average American household has 13 payment cards, including credit cards, debit cards and store cards. There are 1.3 billion payment cards in circulation in the United States.*

- *Americans made $1.1 trillion worth of credit card purchases in 1999.*

- *Americans carry, on average, $5,800 in credit card debt from month to month. If one were to make only the minimum pay-ment on that debt every month, it would take 30 years to pay off — and include an additional $15,000 in interest.*

  For some, digging out of debt proves impossible. According to the American Bankruptcy Institute, 302,829 people filed for bankruptcy in the first quarter of 2000.

Considering these facts alone it makes it easier to understand why we have freely become slaves to debt. For some it may take a miracle; for others it may simply take some persistent reminding that you too can be debt free. You have got to cleanse your mind of all the garbage that you have heard—the garbage that got you into the debt system in the first place. Stop thinking like a slave and learn to speak words of a truly free man—ownership.

I have a cousin who is bound by a slave mindset. He works at Wal-Mart 40 hours each week, and every time he receives his paycheck, the first thing he does is purchase clothes and other items for him and his family in the same store. Then he buys his groceries in the same store. After all his spending, he has only enough money left over for gas and minor upkeep of his car. Note, he does not have a savings account with Wal-Mart, just a Wal-Mart credit card that keeps him in the cycle of debt—slavery. At this rate, my cousin will never be freed.

"Stop thinking like a slave and learn to speak words of a truly free man— ownership."

America—Our In-Debt Example

Added to the already existing problem of personal debt in America is America itself. Every person who has been born in America inherited a debt mindset from the very day he or she came into the world. The reason is obvious. When you were born you became a part of the foot soldiers working tirelessly to help pay off America's lofty debt. I realize you did not create the debt; but, unfortunately, you are going to have to pay the debt.

At the time of this writing the outstanding public debt in the United States of America is $6,471,573,915,690.37 and has already increased millions of dollars as you read these words. The estimated United States population is somewhere around 290,815,710. That means you owe about $22,254. It's my guess that if you were asked to pay off your portion of this debt, you just might not have your share.

Even if you did have the money, I am pretty sure it would already be accounted for in some way. You probably would not want to contribute to pay off a debt that you did not make and probably did not approve of. Perhaps you are an optimist; maybe you are one of those people that think the debt is going to slow down. Think again. The national debt has continually increased on an average of $1.18 billion each day since September 30, 2002. This is a horrible example of overspending; yet, it is reality, and it has become your example.

You can get into debt one of two ways. The most common way is to spend what you do not have money to pay for. It's real simple. If you don't have the money to pay, then borrow the money from your debt card or take a loan and pay later. That's the American way. It is also the pattern that keeps you in slavery. The second way to get into debt is to inherit a debt that you could not prevent. Some examples of this kind of debt would be medical expenses, state and county property taxes, and of course our wonderful deficit.

"Debt is a choice. Face it—it's true."

Most people are deep in debt because they have ignorantly chosen to take the first path as their road to debt slavery. That is something that you are going to have to accept. Debt is a *choice*. Face it—it's true.

No one put a gun to your head and forced you to get a new car with a loan when your old car was still working fine. The two thousand square foot colonial served your purpose well, yet you felt compelled to overextend yourself purchasing a house twice the size. Now your monthly expenses have more than doubled and your property taxes tripled. The only problem is that your annual raise increased your income by a mere five thousand dollars. That was obviously a bad choice. Did you really have to charge an entirely new wardrobe? Last year's wardrobe was still in great shape.

I recognize that the problem is great. Too, I realize that we have a horrible example for how we should spend and how we should conserve. Billions of advertising dollars are spent each year to solidify your bad habit and spend-all thought pattern. Will you continue to be their guinea pig or will you break out of the mold?

Television, the Slave Master

One of the most alluring methods used to enslave American children, adults, and youth is the television. According to the A.C.

Nielsen Co., the average American watches more than four hours of TV each day (or 28 hours per week, or two months of nonstop TV-watching per year). In a 65-year life, a person will have spent nine years glued to the tube. Just think about it for one minute— two solid months of each year are spent watching television.

In one sense it is as if you are enrolled in TU, "Television University." Two solid months equate to more hours than you would spend if you were enrolled full time at a fully accredited university. What do you think is happening all this time while you are watching program after program? You are being taught. What are you being taught? You are being taught how to think. Unfortunately, you are not being taught how to think objectively. It would be wonderful if you were being taught how to think like Christ. That's not the case. You are being taught how they want you to think. You are being taught how to think like a slave of a system.

Primarily most television viewing teaches you two things. The first thing you are being taught is to think anti-life. Of course they know when to start influencing your way of thinking...from the time you are a child. Did you know that before most children finish elementary school they would have witnessed on television more than 8,000 murders? If you think that's bad, by the time a young child reaches 18 years of age they will have watched more than one-fifth of a million acts of violence. Of those acts of violence more than 40,000 will have ended in death.

All this death stuff has to have a negative effect on the human psyche. If you are watching deaths all day long, how can that inspire you to live life to the fullest? Obviously, it cannot. Like begets like. Oranges produce oranges, apples make apples, pears produce pears, people give birth to little people, dogs have puppies, and so on. I think you've got the point. You are bound to become whatever you are taught.

Added to the tremendous influx of violence on television is how we are subliminally coaxed into believing that colas, burgers, fries, and all other fast foods are healthy for us to eat. Unfortunately, far too many people have bought into this lie, which has caused more health problems than we are ready to deal with.

Recently, Surgeon General David Satcher stated that obesity is reaching "epidemic proportions" in the United States and might cause as much preventable disease and death as cigarette smoking. Approximately 61 percent of adults and 14 percent of adolescents have a problem with obesity and about 300,000 die annually from health problems related to obesity. Satcher released a "call to action" to battle a condition he has said should be treated as a disease. However, obesity is not just something that affects the individual; obesity costs the United States $117 billion per year. That's absolutely outrageous!

Dr. Satcher has suggested plans of action to address this crucial issue. Much of his plan centers on changing the food plan in America's public school system that consists mostly of junk food. Although this may be a good place to begin, the problem does not evolve from our school cafeterias. It originates in the homes where the television set has replaced solid instruction from parents. So as long as there are commercials advertising how great "killer food" is for you, you'll keep eating it. In fact, you'll search for it.

On top of all of that are the thousands of drug advertisements that the pharmaceutical companies push on you every time you turn on the television. Although they do not falsely claim that their product will cure you, still most people feel obligated to buy pills that hopefully might give them some temporary relief. And as with any drug, if you take it long enough, your body will become accustomed to the drug and begin to desire it all the time, perpetuating the sickness.

The second thing that Television University teaches you is how to think about money. Advertisers strategically create witty ways to get you to purchase products that you do not have the money to buy. This poor principle teaches you to stay in debt and appreciate it.

You've heard the car commercials before, "No money down, good credit, bad credit, or no credit at all, you can drive away in the car of your dream today!" How stupid can anyone be?

Why would anyone in their right mind *give* someone, who has horrible credit and very little money, a car that is worth fifteen thousand dollars or more? Would you *give* someone fifteen thousand dollars if you knew they had a reputation for never paying money back? Of course you wouldn't. Then why do reputable businesses do so? They don't. They get you into your dream car with supposedly no money down and struggling credit because they are in recruiting season and they have to meet their quotas.

You ask, "What are they recruiting?" They are recruiting strong, red-blooded, hardworking, yet misinformed slaves. And when you sign the dotted line, you become one of their slaves. On average you will earn them from 20 to 25 cents for every dollar that you borrow from them.

Most people with money would lend you their money if they knew they were going to get up to 25 percent on each dollar borrowed. For the lender this makes great business sense. For the borrower this concept should be totally insane. Most people could not get 25-percent interest at the bank, in a mutual fund, or a government bond within the time period of your car loan, which is usually 36 to 60 months. But they can get it from you! You are helping them not only to get rich but also to stay rich, while you get poorer with each paycheck. This insanity has to change.

This liability mindset is the type you will develop when you continue to make television your source of inspiration and instruction. I am not saying there are no worthwhile programs on television today. However, they are but a few; and they are rarely watched. CNN's money programs do not receive anywhere near the ratings that "American Idol" or "Seinfield" receive. Why? People would rather dream and fantasize about becoming rich than to learn proven strategies that produce wealth.

What about the news? Are they a reliable money source? Just use your common sense. Most meteorologists have a difficult time correctly predicting the weather. One day they'll predict that a blizzard is on the way only to experience a 50-degree sunshiny day. Reporters are paid to report on issues in a way that appeals to the greater population in society. They are not paid to investigate truth. In most cases they don't report truth. They report a one-sided, watered-down viewpoint.

Very skillfully and nearly subliminally they will coerce you into believing that debt is a good thing. Instead of frowning at habitual overspending, you will feel good about indebtedness. After all, "You deserve it. You've worked hard for it. Have it your way." I have diagnosed television viewing as a part of the problem that leads to sickness and poverty. Ultimately it causes the viewer to become unproductive and constantly seeking the easy road to riches. Since your physical and financial fitness is directly proportionate to your soul prosperity, you must discipline your mind to start focusing on the things that you can become.

He who has a slack hand becomes poor, but the hand of the diligent makes rich (Proverbs 10:4).

The Borrower Is Servant to the Lender

The rich rules over the poor, and the borrower is servant to the lender (Proverbs 22:7).

I'd like to inspire a thought within you: You will only be as free as you can afford to be. Although in most cases this seems to be outright unjust, it still remains a fact. You have to begin to view debt as your archenemy and most of all as an enemy to true freedom. The more you owe, the less free you are. You will always live in servitude to the one whom you owe money to.

The welfare system is a system that creates total loyalty to the one who gives out the check. Once you receive welfare money, you begin to think like a welfare recipient, act like you are needy, and always look to others to free you from your present difficult situation. This is true because *the borrower is servant to the lender.* You say, "I never borrowed a dime from the state that I live in. They freely gave me the money." Think again.

When your mother or father gave you money as a child to buy ice cream or candy, do you remember ever filling out an application to qualify for the money they were giving to you? Did you have to sign a piece of paper agreeing to any terms as a basis for receiving the candy money? I am sure you did not. You might think this example sounds a little foolish, but there is a valid point here.

> *"You will always live in servitude to the one whom you owe money to."*

Applications and paperwork are always required to get any type of assistance. They do this, not for your benefit, but as a written record of how much money they gave you (really lent you) and for how long. They want to know this just in case you ever get in a position of wealth; they (the state that funded you the loan under the guise of assistance) are going to get their money (the loan that you did not realize was a loan) paid back in full.

Real gifts in life do not require paperwork to be signed; but in our modern culture, all loans require substantial paperwork to be completed before any money is issued. The paperwork is proof that you willingly signed away your rights to a system. You became a servant to the one who offered the money to you. Until you are out of debt, you will always be in bondage to some extent.

Even if you are not on welfare or state assistance, debt on any level continues to make you a servant to who you borrowed from. When I closed on my first home, I read every single word on my closing documents. I happened to notice that one page was dedicated to informing me on how I should take care of the property. Most of the things listed were things that any sensible homeowner would want to do anyway.

The Total Package

The point is this: If I as the homeowner did not comply with the "how to" list concerning the overall upkeep of the property, the bank (the lender) could use property neglect as a valid and contractual reason to foreclose on my (the servant) property. Who gave them this authority? I gave them the authority when I chose to sign a document agreeing to the lender's terms.

Are you saying that I should never get a loan for a car or home? No, that's not what I am saying at all. Realistically, such provisions can be a blessing to a person who does not have a couple hundred thousand dollars just sitting around. The message I am trying to get you to understand is that until you have become free of debt, you are not totally free. And freedom should always be our ultimate goal.

Get Out of Debt

Having said all of that, the very first thing you need to do is STOP your credit spending. All credit spending will only exacerbate your situation. Each time you pull out your credit card you are killing your chances of becoming wealthy. You are also increasing the time period that you have agreed to be a servant to the lender.

Start spending your money now on the things that you need in order to survive, such as food (not an overabundance), clothing (not extreme in this area), and shelter (the best that your money can afford). Understandably you are going to have to pay for the upkeep and utilities associated with your house. But that's all. Any extras must be kept on hold until you are able to at least see the promised land. Later, I'll note in greater detail an actual plan of action for your debt elimination. But for now, cut up those credit cards, and learn the ancient lost art of saying "*no.*"

Endnote

1. "CardFAQ's—Frequently Asked Questions: Statistics." *CardWeb.com,* CardWeb.com, Inc., 1986–2003. June 12, 2003. <http://www.CardWeb.com/cardlearn/stat.html>.

Chapter Three

Displaced Priorities

There is a time for everything, and a season for every activity under heaven: a time to be born and a time to die, a time to plant and a time to uproot, a time to kill and a time to heal, a time to tear down and a time to build, a time to weep and a time to laugh, a time to mourn and a time to dance, a time to scatter stones and a time to gather them, a time to embrace and a time to refrain, a time to search and a time to give up, a time to keep and a time to throw away, a time to tear and a time to mend, a time to be silent and a time to speak, a time to love and a time to hate, a time for war and a time for peace (Ecclesiastes 3:1-8 NIV).

In Ecclesiastes chapter 3 Solomon so eloquently deals with the issue of time and timing. The Scripture opens up exclaiming, "*There is a time for everything, and a season for every activity under heaven.*" I believe that by understanding this, you will more easily be able to understand just how to place matters of priority in your life. There is a time for everything, which means there is a time to purchase and a time to refrain from purchasing. Whether an item is on sale or not does not matter as to whether you should buy. Proper timing should always outweigh all other factors when making buying decisions.

There are times to borrow and times when borrowing is totally unacceptable no matter what. There are times to invest and there are times when investing needs to be thought through a little more thoroughly. It is important for you to know when to save and when to make the needed withdrawal. Everything I am saying amounts to knowing where to place your priorities.

Noted author Dr. Myles Munroe once said, "Never let what matters most suffer at the expense of the things that matters the least." The point is that everything matters. You must determine what matters more than others. Having that kind of insight does not come easily nor does it come overnight. It takes skill and discipline to discover and discern the proper times and season to act or refrain from acting at all.

There are many levels of stock investors. You have beginner investors whose knowledge of the market is very shallow; hence they will often try to make investments where there is the least potential for loss. The highly skilled investors who are most savvy and usually high-risk takers did not become as knowledgeable as they are by sheer luck. They don't make hopeful guesses concerning multiple millions of dollars. On the contrary, they have become experts at knowing when to buy and when to sell. As complicated as the market may appear to be to the uninitiated soul, knowing when to buy from when to sell or hold is the whole science of stocks in a nutshell.

These highly skilled investors have become the masters of self-discipline. They have their priorities in proper place. No matter what, they continue to stick to the rules they have set in place for their own selves. Consequently, this type of investor seems to be profitable regardless of whether the market reports losses or gains.

As a matter of fact, they tend to earn even greater dividends when the market is doing extremely poorly.

So their prosperity is not only connected to having the right kind of knowledge but also to prioritizing the method or plan of action that will work best in various given scenarios. By using that example, you too can see gains in nearly every area of your life once you have learned to put your life in its proper place.

What Matters Most?

Ask yourself the question, "Of all the things that money can buy, which one of those things matter the most?" The answer to this question is crucial, because it will determine exactly where your heart is. *"For where your treasure is, there your heart will be also"* (Mt. 6:21). Where your heart is ultimately tells where your priorities are, whether they are good or bad.

Today if you were given a check for five thousand dollars, what would you do with it? Would you spend it all in one day? Would you purchase new clothing for you or your children? Maybe you would invest at least some of the money. Perhaps you might decrease your present debts by paying off some pressing bills. You might give a large offering to your church so that you can plant some seed money in good soil expecting the blessing that flows from your heart of obedience. Just for a moment, honestly consider what you would do with the money.

What you would do with the money determines what matters most to you. What I have discovered is that most people have displaced priorities in life. Although their hearts may be sincere, their judgment is horrible and grossly unprofitable. Although the following scenario may sound like one that is far-fetched, it may be closer to your reality than you actually realize.

Millions of taxpayers receive an income tax check from the government each year. Some checks may not be as substantial as others. However, it is known that most people who do not earn enough money throughout the course of the year to exceed the set poverty level will receive far more money on their income tax return check than people who earn greater incomes. If those same people who earn below the set poverty levels have children, each child will afford them an earned income credit, which is a government tax favor that considers the cost of providing for your children's expense and gives the taxpayer leniency based on that fact.

I've seen people receive three, four, five, and as much as eight thousand dollars as an income tax refund. These same people, due to grossly displaced priorities and mass mismanagement, often owe nearly twice the amount and in some case three times the amount of their refund in debts. Just put your priority thinking cap on for a minute. Wouldn't it make high priority sense to use that money to decrease your total debt between 50 to 70 percent? I think so.

Using this simple financial logic, in less than three years time, you could be totally debt free. And if you would still qualify to receive an income tax refund check in your fourth year of your debt decreasing process, you could use the money for investment purposes or purchase the things you may desire using cash. Although this dream could become a reality, for most people in this situation it doesn't seem to work out this way.

Just the opposite happens. You may receive between four to five thousand dollars on your income tax return. Then instead of decreasing your debt obligations, you party. You spend lavishly on your friends, your children, other family members, and of course those who you are intentionally trying to impress. The end result is being more deeply entrenched in debt and the sorrow that goes along with debt. The solution is in knowing what matters most and tending to those things first.

You ask, "How can I know what matters most? After all, if I do not know what my priorities should be, then I won't recognize when

40

I am making a good or bad decision." In two to five minutes I can tell you exactly what matters most to you. That answer is in your checkbook if you have one. If you don't use checks, then the answer is probably in your check card statement, VISA, MasterCard, American Express statement, or your ATM monthly register.

"In two to five minutes I can tell you exactly what matters most to you. That answer is in your checkbook..."

If you are a strictly cash-and-carry type of person, then I will be able to get all the information about you from your cash receipts. Now if you tell me that you don't have any of the above, then it's obvious that your lack of order is the main reason why you are in the situation you are in. Hopefully that is not your case. To simplify my argument let's just say that you regularly use a checkbook for all your purchases.

From your checkbook, I can tell within the first two to three pages what matters most to you—where your priorities are. If you are a drinker, then I am sure I'll see various lines with checks made payable to your favorite package store. If buying books and audio teaching tapes are your fancy, then I'm sure I'll see places like Borders, Waldenbooks, Barnes and Noble, Books a Million, and Amazon.com on your balance ledger.

If you absolutely adore buying clothes, then I know that I'll see several major clothing stores on your balances. Perhaps you know someone who suffers with a drug addiction. Well, that person will spend enormous amounts of money to support his or her habit. In the same manner, if you really love God and His Church, it too will be reflected by your generous tithes and offering giving. Whatever you love, it will be on your priority list to sow into or to purchase. It's only human nature.

Here's the problem: Far too many people have put the trivial things first on their "to buy" list. What I mean by trivial things is things such as designer clothing, regularly eating out, going on fantasy vacations, buying late model cars (to keep up with the Jones), and any other items that will make people believe you are well to do. I'll talk more about that in the next section.

The bottom line for now is knowing how to put your money in places where it counts. Here is the rule of thumb—purchase (put the bulk of your money into) things that have the potential to increase in value. Real estate increases in value. Mutual funds, government bonds, and stocks all have potential to increase in value. Businesses, if run properly, will always increase in value, yielding a far greater return than your initial investment. When you do things such as these, you are placing your priorities in the right place.

Putting your priorities in the right place is not only profitable in the financial arena, but it is also equally profitable to your health. Just recently, I called a sheetrock contractor named Ken. About six years ago he skim coated a wall at our previous church location. Since he did a pretty good job I asked him to give me an estimate on some skim coating work that needed to be done at my new home.

I clearly remember six years ago when Ken was working for me, he would leave our sanctuary to take long smoke breaks. During his hour to an hour-and-a-half smoke breaks he would smoke nearly two packs of cigarettes without stopping to take a breath. As a health crusader, I felt it was my responsibility to at least let him know that this habit was going to kill him if he continued in this manner.

Like many, he sort of shrugged me off, clearly informing me that he would have to die of something anyway. He asked, "Why not cigarettes?" He said, "Some folks die of old age, others get killed, some die from drinking too much. I guess I'll die from smoking. What's the big deal?" Needless to say, I felt pretty bad for him.

By the confession of his own mouth I detected that his values were obviously displaced. His habit wasn't my greatest worry. I knew and still do know that there are millions of people who have an addictive smoking habit. What bothered me most was his ignorance concerning the present and future state of his health. No matter what I told him he just did not seem to care. That really bothered me.

A few days after I called him, he returned my call. Regretfully, he informed me that he could not work for me. He went on to say that he was unable to hang sheetrock or skim coat walls ever again. Naturally I asked him why he could not work anymore. He told me that he had had two major heart attacks and a minor stroke all within a 30-day period. His doctor told him that it is a miracle that he is even alive.

Due to the severity of his condition and the weak state that his heart is in he cannot work again—ever. Working, whether light industrial or heavy work, would cause him to die instantly. Not wanting to chance this, he agreed to give up the profession that he loved so dearly. Before our conversation ended, he proudly confessed to me that he had given up cigarette smoking forever. What helped him to come to this decision was that his doctor told him that his smoking habit severely weakened both his heart and lungs.

If he were to continue smoking, he would be dead within three months. What amazed me was how easily he was able to kick the habit when he realized that his life would come to a quick and sudden end. To my total surprise he now wants to know everything I know about proper eating and living a highly health-conscious lifestyle.

After the conversation had ended I was quite amazed by his sudden change of heart. All kinds of questions twirled around in my mind. I had previously given him what I thought were valid reasons to kick the habit. Why couldn't he kick the habit before? The answer became clear. He couldn't kick the habit before because he had displaced priorities.

He had poured his finances and energy into his addictive habit. Just imagine what his life could have been like had he heeded my warning nearly six years ago. It is very possible that he could have totally averted his heart attacks and stroke. He could have totally rebuilt and renewed his body, making it a complete model of health in a six-year stretch. Like millions of other people, he chose to invest in a lower priority that ultimately ruined his livelihood and nearly cost his life.

"Most Americans invest into things that matter the least."

What Matters Least?

Although it does not always work out like this, what should matter least is anything that does not have the potential to either earn you money or provide the basic needs to live well in life. Anything that does not have appreciation value should be on the bottom of your priority list. The poor are poor in many cases because they often major in the minors. They want to look the part. They want to appear to have money so they purchase clothing that will make people believe they are rich although they are bum broke.

Most Americans invest into things that matter the least. Maybe these things matter to them, but in terms of building lasting wealth they don't contribute. It always freaks me out when I see a late model Mercedes Benz parked in front of an apartment, or worse, in front of the housing projects. I'll be the first to admit that Mercedes Benz manufactures one of the world's finest vehicles. However, most of their cars are not equipped with a futon, a full bath, or a kitchen. Since they aren't, driving a Mercedes Benz should be a very low priority for any non-homeowner.

You have to start putting things in their proper perspective. First purchase a home. Then purchase the car that compliments your home. For example if you live in a house that's worth about $80,000, why would you drive a car that is worth $130,000 before the luxury and gas guzzler taxes are added on? Somehow this equation does not seem to balance.

Displaced Priorities

Put first things first. Comparing money to health, your health is always far greater than financial wealth. That is putting first things first. I have clients who work many hours trying to get ahead financially, yet they do not take out the necessary time to take care of their body. What will your money be worth to you when you are dead? For starters, you can have a pretty cool funeral procession with all of the expensive trappings. The sad thing is, you won't be able to enjoy it.

I realize that I am being a bit sardonic, but I am trying to get you to understand my point. In order for you to live life to its fullest and in order for you to have this "total package," you must have balance. You cannot neglect either side of the coin. Your total package can be likened to a coin that has two sides. One side is health, the other is wealth. You need both.

What would your life be like if you had great health yet you were financially poor? There wouldn't be too many places that you could travel abroad. You wouldn't be able to bless others. How would you be able to help those who are in need of food, clothing, and shelter? Face it, you couldn't help them because all those things require money.

On the other hand, you could have shiploads of money yet suffer with a supposedly incurable disease. What good is your money then? You cannot buy health. You can purchase things that will help you maintain good health such as vitamins, minerals, a great naturopathic doctor, a chiropractor, a gym subscription, and pure drinking water. But you cannot buy health itself.

Since you cannot buy health and health is a high priority, you have to do things that will create good health in you. Regarding financial matters, you can buy stocks, businesses, bonds, or property. All of those things can be exchanged for your money. Good health has much to do with knowing what and what not to receive into your body. Like the skilled stockbroker, in time you will intuitively know how to discern what is best for your body. It begins with prioritizing.

The Total Package

What Doesn't Matter at All?

There are some things that matter greatly; there are some things that matter a little; and there are some things that shouldn't matter at all. When faced with things that don't matter at all, it should be relatively easy to just move on. The only reason you would not be able to move on is if those things that should not matter at all, have become a high priority or addiction in your life.

Billions of dollars are spent each year on gambling. It would make sense to me if the billions of dollars spent were generated from the accounts of billionaires. Unfortunately, this is not true. The billions of dollars generated come from poor folks with high expectations of becoming rich through gambling. Let's suppose that all of the people who are relatively low-income earners pooled their monies together to open up a business. Let's say the business is a publishing business.

This business would have enough start-up revenue to position itself to be the fasting growing business in the world, securing the number one spot amongst Fortune 500 companies in the United States. Let's say that this company went public and began to sell stocks to interested investors. They would get millions of investors to invest primarily because the company quickly proved that it could become tremendously profitable in a record amount of time.

All of the once poor, high hoping gamblers would suddenly become multimillionaires, never having to worry about money again. Unfortunately my scenario is fictitious and will probably never happen. For people who are poor, gambling should never be an option. If you don't have money enough to meet your needs, why would you consider gambling what little you have away?

Another way that people invest in things that do not matter is by using their money to enable other people to become unfruitful and unproductive. Have you ever heard of the word *enabler*? An enabler supports the dysfunctional behavior of another person.

They do so by financially or morally supporting a person's habit or by denying that the behavior exists at all.

You commonly see this behavior in relationships where a person is on drugs and that person has a mother, sister, grandmother, or friend who enables or supports their addiction by giving them money, buying them clothes, feeding them, and giving them a place to stay. Not only does this type of assistance perpetuate negative behavior on the part of the addict; it is grossly, financially, and emotionally draining to the person who is playing the role of God.

Supporting someone else's addictive behavior should not matter at all to you. Yet so many people take on a responsibility that is not theirs. Some mothers have been notorious for retarding the development of their male children by allowing them to live irresponsibly while the mothers pay for every mistake that their sons make. This too becomes a financial drain in time.

You have to recognize that there are some things that do not matter. And if they don't matter, then those things do not need any of your time or attention—and they certainly don't need your money. As you continue to read you will be given hands-on, how-to formulas for getting out of debt, building wealth, and of course walking in divine health. You should become accustomed with words like *prevention* and *planning*, both of which are necessary to use if you want to be healthy and wealthy.

Knowing the Condition You Are in Now

Considering all that you have just read you need to honestly know where you stand now. In order to do that, I have provided some blank spaces below for you to fill in. Understand that there are right and wrong answers. But for this exercise, let's say there are not. I want you to get a realistic idea of the condition you are in now. If you don't know where you are, it is going to be difficult to move forward.

The Total Package

So this exercise is one that will help you to not only see where you are but also to help position where you need to be, ultimately pointing you in the right direction. I have listed three categories: High Priorities, Low Priorities, and those things that Shouldn't Matter. I want you to take your time and think of at least seven things that will fit each of the three categories listed. Be honest and do it now!

High Priorities	Low Priorities	Shouldn't Matter

If you are trying to cheat, don't. Get your pencil out and do the assignment. If you have filled in all the blanks, I commend you. Now what you need to do is make some adjustments based on the information that I have given to you.

On the graph below, I want you to place the same things that you have already printed on the chart above in their rightful places. The categories below are: Things That Make Money, Things Needed to Live, and Things That Take Money away from you. Do it now—the results should be interesting.

Things That Make Money	Things Needed to Live	Things That Take Money

Displaced Priorities

As I have said before, most all these principles can be applied to both the wealth and health areas. Now complete the health chart below. I want you to get an idea of the simple changes you can make to improve your life in an enormous way.

Concerning my health:

Things I Need to Do	Habits I Need to Quit	What to Eat	What Not to Eat

The Total Package

Part 2

The Prognosis

"A forecast or forecasting; esp., a prediction of the probable course of a disease in an individual and the chances of recovery."

Chapter Four

Health and Wealth—A State of Mind

For as he thinks within himself, so he is (Proverbs 23:7a NAS).

As we move from the diagnosis to the prognosis there are a few things that you must know before we can perform surgery on your financial condition and give biblical prescriptions for your health and wholeness. First, you are what you think. The future of your finances will depend greatly on how you think about finances. How you think about money determines whether you will ever have it or not.

Every Christian believer's goal should be to think like Jesus would think. How would Jesus think about money if He lived in a capitalistic society? What would Jesus think of HMO's and the present crisis in our healthcare system? Would Jesus live like a pauper or would He live like the King that He is? Would Jesus care about having a thriving economy or would He just want His people to move to the mountains and escape the day-to-day realities of city dwellers? The point is, whatever Jesus would do is what we should do. Equally, how He would think is exactly how we should want to align our thought processes as well.

There are so many opinions, theologies, and theories about what Jesus thought about money. Some believe that Jesus was a very poor man while on earth and that His poorness contributed to the quality of holiness that He so humbly possessed. Others believe that Jesus was filthy rich, that He wore the finest clothing that money could buy, ate choice epicurean delights, and traveled first class wherever His Father sent Him. Then there are many others who confess that they do not have an opinion. They simply admit that they just don't know whether He was poor, rich, or in between. Irregardless of what you think, I would like to help dispel any negative thought processes about money, which you may have adopted by association with or assimilation into this world's system.

A Critical Analysis of Stinking Thinking

Although I dislike generalizing, I have to say the majority of people in this country seem to have a rather cynical view about money. Worse yet is their cynicism toward whom has the money. And yet, there are certain people in society that the "cynics" have approved as being worthy of receiving and having a whole lot of money. For example, people who are famous television personalities are allowed in most people's thinking to have as much money as they desire.

Very seldom will you hear someone say, "Twenty million dollars is too much for comedian Jim Carey to earn for one movie." When was the last time you heard someone criticize basketball stars Allen Iverson, Shaquille O'neal, or Ray Allen for making too much money? You probably haven't. In recent months you probably have not heard of anyone on an all-out campaign to limit the earnings of stock investors' investments.

For the most part, movie stars, entertainers, comedians, profes-sional athletes, and those who hold seats on the New York Stock Exchange are expected to prosper financially. No one seems to mind. Quite honestly, no one should mind, because they all are earn-ing wages based on performance. A lousy performance amounts to zero wages earned. Exceptional performance is rewarded with exceptional earnings and a possible bonus. So there are some in socie-ty who we expect to have financial riches.

"...the richer you are the less you care about who has what...

We don't mind if they live in palatial homes, drive exotic cars, fly first class, stay in five-star hotels and resorts, and regularly go on dream vacations. In our mind, they are supposed to live that way. However, when a minister, for example, or a pastor, or bishop, lives a lifestyle of abundance, their credibility and integrity are immediately questioned. "That preacher must be taking all the money," you'll hear them say. When you hear thoughtless statements like this, you can come to the con-clusion that the person saying it probably lacks money.

The poor, on the other hand, tend to have all the time in the world to wonder about other people."

Many of my clients are very wealthy people. Some have been investing their money before I was even born; others started within the past few years. One of the things that I have noticed is, the rich-er you are the less you care about who has what. Rich folks are not a threat to your riches. Rich people for the most part are too busy trying to secure their own nest eggs, which means they really don't have time to monitor or even care about what you are doing.

The poor, on the other hand, tend to have all the time in the world to wonder about other people. They especially scrutinize the lives of visible local figures, such as pastors. But stinking thinking would suggest that a preacher should be poor. There is not one

Scripture in the entire Bible that would substantiate this falsehood, but unfortunately, people continue to think that the preacher should be poor.

From my observations, most people who feel and think this way are poor themselves. Somehow they erroneously believe that if the minister is rich, he has done something illegal or immoral to achieve his financial wealth. The truth is that for the most part, if a pastor is rich, it is because he has sown much seed and is experiencing a great harvest in direct proportion to his giving.

Consistency is key to any area of growth in life. Los Angeles Lakers star Kobe Bryant did not wake up one day, gifted with the know-how and skills to be the basketball champion that he is. Bryant like any other great basketball player had to commit to rigorous exercise and daily practice of foul shooting, dribbling, and shooting jump shots. That's how he grew into the player that he is now. Although he is still young, it did not happen overnight for him. It took time.

When people acquire wealth, barring that the money was stolen, there has to have been consistency on the part of the steward to manage the money in order to gain more. I'm sure you have heard people suggest that a preacher is taking all the money. But think about it for a moment: If any pastor took all the money that came in the offering plate to use for his or her own personal use, how then would the bills get paid?

Let's say that the church has a mortgage. Who then would pay the mortgage? Who would pay for the electricity and the heating expenses? Who would pay for the general upkeep of the building? If the church has paid staff, how would their salaries be paid? How about the high costs of church liability insurance, auto insurance for the church vehicles, and health premiums? I guess those expenses just get paid through prayer and fasting.

What I have just noted is only an abridged listing of the multiple expenditures that it takes to run a church successfully. Yet you hear ill-advised and empty, disparaging remarks about ministers and finances all the time. The person spewing out the remarks always proves by his own comments that he has been infected with the stinking thinking virus. And it is this virus that clutches its victims in a prison of poverty and lack.

So you must begin to change your thinking. If you are born again, you should sincerely desire that your minister and family be well taken care of. You need to recognize that if your minister experiences prosperity, then you too will experience prosperity if you are properly aligned. It should not matter to you what another man has.

I have heard people say of preachers, businessmen, and politicians, "There's no reason for them to have all that money when there are so many poor people in the world." Why are statements like these stinking thinking? Think about it. If the rich individual decreases his salary to fit your opinion of what you believe he deserves to make, will that actually alleviate the condition of poverty? Of course it won't.

Poverty is birthed in a mix of various factors. Some of those factors are regional, political, environmental, or economical. An evil political regime will inevitably apply unnecessary pressure and burden on the people. That by itself will produce widespread poverty. Polytheistic nations such as India and China have experienced poverty, in my opinion, because of their rejection of the gospel of the Kingdom.

It is the gospel of the Kingdom that produces wealth. Wherever its message is heralded the opportunity for prosperity increases vastly. On the flip side wherever its message is banned, poverty will come quickly. In some countries, rain is scarce and the land cannot produce vegetation. Where there is no rain, there is no food. Where there is no food, there is no livestock. The citizens in those countries will eventually become very unhealthy because everything that is living depends on water to survive.

The Total Package

So whether "Mr. Rich" drives a Rolls Royce, Mercedes Benz, Lexus, or BMW does not matter. What he drives or where he lives is not going to change how people live in Ethiopia or Mozambique. Even if he gave all his money to the people of a poverty-stricken country, it wouldn't cure the problem.

Consider another example: "Mr. Broke Don Carr" drives a piece of junk that barely works. The muffler on his car has fallen off and now his car is spewing out toxic carcinogens into the air causing potential death to millions. Obviously he is saving all the money he has earned because he does not want people to think that he identifies with the affluent group of society. However, all the money that he is saving is not helping anybody, not even himself obviously.

So is there a real point in claiming that the rich are always taking from the poor? In some situations, but not all. In the United States of America that argument holds far less weight than it does in an unindustrialized nation. In this country the rich cannot directly take away from the poor for obvious reasons. The poor have nothing to give.

Because of my genuine concern for God's people, I give money to the foreign mission fields on a regular basis. I also intentionally try to support domestic mission organizations such as "Larry Jones Feed the Children" and foreign mission organizations such as Save Africa's Children-Pan African Children's Fund. You may contact them on the web at www.saveafricaschildren.org or by writing Save Africa's Children, P.O. Box 8386, Los Angeles, CA 90008-0386. My giving helps to feed a family or even families. When I do this, I am obeying the Word of God. I am part of fulfilling a greater commission to feed the hungry, clothe the naked, and shelter the homeless.

Then the righteous will answer Him, saying, "Lord, when did we see You hungry and feed You, or thirsty and give You drink?"...And the King will answer and say to them,

"Assuredly, I say to you, inasmuch as you did it to one of the least of these My brethren, you did it to Me" (Matthew 25:37,40).

However, when I give I don't believe that I am changing the situation of poverty or eradicating the plight of the poor. That job is a job for God. It can only be done through and by His Spirit. In the same manner that a believer must repent—change his or her mind before he or she can truly be saved—you must change your mindset about prosperity. Even where governmental corruption does not exist and famine has not touched the land, poverty still makes its home in the mind (the thinking) of billions of people. Until that mindset changes, we will always have the poor with us.

A Costly Lesson

And being in Bethany at the house of Simon the leper, as He sat at the table, a woman came having an alabaster flask of very costly oil of spikenard. Then she broke the flask and poured it on His head. But there were some who were indignant among themselves, and said, "Why was this fragrant oil wasted? For it might have been sold for more than three hundred denarii and given to the poor." And they criticized her sharply. But Jesus said, "Let her alone. Why do you trouble her? She has done a good work for Me. For you have the poor with you always, and whenever you wish you may do them good; but Me you do not have always. She has done what she could. She has come beforehand to anoint My body for burial. Assuredly, I say to you, wherever this gospel is preached in the whole world, what this woman has done will also be told as a memorial to her" (Mark 14:3-9).

The Total Package

Here is a classic Bible story about a woman who wanted to bless King Jesus with a very costly gift. When Jesus was at Simon's home she came to Him while He was sitting at Simon's table. Knowing who Jesus was and realizing that this opportunity may never come again for her, she broke the seal on an extremely expensive bottle of fragrant oil and began pouring it on Jesus' head.

Even as many people today believe that it is not worthwhile to be a significant blessing to spiritual shepherds, people then also thought that this woman was crazy for "*wasting*" a precious oil on Jesus. They called her investment in Jesus a waste or unprofitable. Does that train of thought sound a bit familiar to you? Little did any of them perceive that you could never invest too much into God or into the things of God. The returns are phenomenal both in this life and in ages to come. Obviously they did not realize this.

So they did what any low-thinking, ill-informed person would do; they criticized her harshly. "Why did you waste all of that oil? You must be absolutely crazy. Are you out of your living mind? Do you realize how much money that oil was worth? Who's going to replace the oil? What a fool!" These are some of the negative remarks that she may have heard hurled against her, simply because she wanted to be a tangible blessing to Jesus.

They then informed her of exactly how much this bottle of oil was worth. The oil was the equivalent to one year's salary in her time. Can you imagine giving one year's worth of your salary to Jesus? Would He be worth it, or would you think it was a waste? They like people today tried to justify better ways that this offering could have been used. They informed her that she could have sold the bottle and used the proceeds to help the poor.

After Jesus heard this, He told them to leave her alone. *Alone* is a word that represents two words, *all* and *one*. Like many English words, over the years and with much casual usage, these two words have been abbreviated to *alone*. I believe that Jesus may have been trying to convey a message to her critics rather than just chase them away.

Unlike the crowd who had many opinions about money and its worth, this woman was "all one." In other words, she did not have to think twice about her offering because she was already convinced that she was making the right choice. Have you ever been prompted by the Holy Spirit to give a certain amount of money, but then your pew partner, family member, or perhaps a friend began to offer you reasons why you shouldn't give so liberally?

Well, that has happened to me several times. When it has occurred, my thinking overruled their opinion because I was *all one* on the matter. My mind was already made up and nothing could change it. Those who can be talked out of tithing, giving offerings, investing, saving, or even going into business are not one. Unfortunately, those kinds of people are weak-minded people who need others to validate them in some sort of way. They need other people to affirm their behavior. Sadly, they can't make a decision and commit to it unless the "crowd" gives them resounding approval. They are not all one. In fact, the Bible has a term for those kind of people: They are double minded in all their ways. The person who is double, triple, or multi-minded will never receive anything of value because he does not have oneness of purpose.

> But let him ask in faith, with no doubting, for he who doubts is like a wave of the sea driven and tossed by the wind. For let not that man suppose that he will receive anything from the Lord; he is a double-minded man, unstable in all his ways (James 1:6-8).

Jesus told them to leave her *all one*—alone. If they had kept pressuring her, it may have negatively influenced her right way of thinking. Internalizing negative comments are often the beginning of stinking thinking.

Then Jesus makes a very interesting statement, *"For you have the poor with you always, and whenever you wish you may do them good."* Was Jesus promoting poverty? Might Jesus have been praising the state of lack, homelessness, inadequate food and supplies, and vulnerability to disease that many poverty-stricken people suffer from? I don't think so. Jesus was expressing the truth that the poverty mindset is not going to fade away. It will be here until He returns.

You can be financially well-to-do, yet have poverty thinking. There are many examples all around us. This costly price of the lesson was not represented by the value of the ointment that can be replaced. The costly price is how much will be lost in life if one refuses to change their thinking. What will be lost cannot be compared to a year's worth of wages; it is far most costly.

This woman gave an offering that memorialized her until this very day. Her critics are not even named. There are no stories written to honor them. No one knows who they were, what they did, or what contributions (if any) they made to society. Hence, their words are as a vapor. This lesson declares that true financial poverty is not as much about what's in your hand as it is about what's in your head.

How Millionaires Think

Television, rap, R&B, and rock videos tend to sensationalize and over-exaggerate the lifestyles of the rich. They portray images of the rich owning fleets of cars, Lear jets, mansions and Caribbean villa hideaways, million-dollar racehorses, and twenty thousand-dollar show dogs. Inside these rich folks' closets are 365 different outfits, one for each day of the year, of course.

Although there are some (few) rich people who live this ostentatiously, this type of lifestyle does not represent the majority of rich people in the U.S.A. The problem is that television creates an illusion of grandeur, an illusion that these things alone represent real wealth. Consequently, broke folks ignorantly pursue the appearance of riches and financial stability rather than wealth itself.

Why is this not good? You foolishly chase dreams without sleep. You live life in a fantasy world. When you finally come to your senses, you realize that you have spent several years helping the rich to become richer (while your net worth decreases), not through their alleged evil acts, but through your own ignorance. The real truth is that the majority of millionaires do not live as lavish and spend-easy as people may think.

For the most part, millionaires think differently than people in lower economic classes. In their *New York Times* best-selling book, *The Millionaire Next Door: Surprising Secrets of America's Wealthy*, authors Thomas J. Stanley and William D. Danko point out that most millionaires live well below their means, which is one of the main ingredients in obtaining and maintaining wealth. During their research they discovered that the average millionaire displays great frugality in his buying decisions.

"...most millionaires live well below their means, which is one of the main ingredients in obtaining and maintaining wealth."

In their work they've noted some very interesting finds:

Being frugal is the cornerstone of wealth building. Yet far too often the big spenders are promoted and sensationalized by the popular press. But the lavish lifestyle sells TV time and newspapers. All too often young people are indoctrinated with the belief that those who have money spend lavishly and if you don't show it, you don't have it. Could you imagine the media hyping the frugal lifestyle of the typical American millionaire?

The Total Package

What would the results be? Low TV ratings and lack of readership, because most people who build wealth in America are hardworking, thrifty, and not all glamorous. Wealth is rarely gained through the lottery, with a home run, or in a quiz show fashion. But these are the rare jackpots that the press sensationalizes.[1]

Although I am not opposed to living life well, most millionaires choose to purchase items that they can realize their savings on. They don't intentionally try to buy things just for show. In many senses they are *purpose-driven buyers*. What they purchase must serve a particular purpose well. That is why millionaires tend to be performance driven rather than name-brand driven when it comes to making purchases. This makes a lot of sense—dollars and cents.

Did you know that your average millionaire...

- Does not purchase custom-made clothing.

- Does not wear $1000 and above suits.

- Wears shoes that cost $140 or less.

- Does not wear alligator or crocodile print shoes.

- Does not wear gaudy and expensive jewelry.

- Does not have a specialty store credit card.

- Drives an American-made vehicle, not a foreign luxury car.

- Has not spent more than $30,000 for a car throughout his lifetime.

- Lives in a home nearly 20 years (to build up equity and pay off his or her mortgage note).

Perhaps that is why they become millionaires. If you spend all your money and never invest, you will always be broke. Millionaires think in terms of manifested wealth, their portfolio and passive incomes, and real property. They are not fascinated with acquiring a whole lot of stuff just for the sake of it. Think about it: Would you rather own a brand-new $120,000 Mercedes Benz or would you rather own $120,000 worth of Mercedes Benz stock? If you think like the wealthy, your answer is obviously the stock.

The stock has the potential to increase in value. The car loses its value immediately after it is purchased. Even though Mercedes Benz holds their value far greater than most other vehicles, it still is an investment that will decrease like any other vehicle. Who then should own such a fine quality car? The person who can afford the car should own it. By this I mean they should not only be able to afford the purchase of the vehicle, but also the taxes, insurance, and regular maintenance on the car. You also should have money to cover emergency repairs.

Making Los Angeles my home for more than ten years has been a wonderful and financially rewarding experience. However there is a pretentious side to living in Los Angeles that I have noticed over the years. Because of the preponderance of Hollywood glamour it seems that most people are preoccupied with image. Many people have to have the latest model cars, newest clothing lines, and the largest estates.

The problem is that for the most part, it's all pretentious. Others may call it "fronting," putting on an act. How silly is it to drive a late model Lexus, BMW, or Mercedes Benz and then drive to the gas station to put a mere five dollars in the tank because you don't have the money to fill it up? That's insane. Yet I see this all the time. If their car were to break down, most of these *pretenders* would not be able to afford to have the car fixed.

And so the car has to stay in the shop for several weeks until they hustle up the money. Then they are charged additional daily storage fees all because they don't have enough money to really afford such a car. This image thing has gotten most of their minds out of control. They charge (to the limit) high-fashion clothes to appear rich, but they cannot make the very first installment for the charges they make.

These pretenders charge breakfast, lunch, and dinner. They charge face-lifts and other types of plastic surgery. Their fitness center subscriptions are usually charged also. These same desirous souls are usually the ones whose vehicles are repossessed, houses are foreclosed on, and credit card privileges are revoked permanently. Why? They go through such embarrassment only because they refuse to be honest and real about their wealth. While they think they look rich, they really look stupid in the final analysis.

How do the truly rich people think? The rich think in terms of acquiring wealth. They consciously repudiate anything that has the potential to take wealth away from them. This list includes expensive clothing that does not appreciate in value. It includes high interest credit cards, loans, and lines of equity. It includes the long list of things that create an image yet fail to create the *real* wealth that should accompany such an image. They don't care what you think about them or what your opinion is of them. Their lives are not dictated by what the media believes they should have or how advertisers think they should live.

The bottom line is that they live by these philosophies: Spend less than what you make; after your expenses and liabilities are satisfied, invest what remains—always invest! It does not matter whether you can scrape up enough money to own the house. Can you afford to maintain everything else that goes along with owning the house? This same train of thought goes for owning a car, a yacht, a vacation home, a timeshare, or a club membership. You may have the initial investment, but can you keep it up? That's the question that the rich ask, that the poor do not.

How Do You Feel Today?

Inasmuch as wealth is a state of mind, healing and being healthy is also a state of mind. Some may ask, "Is it truly as simple as just thinking or believing that you are healthy in order to be healthy?" Your thought life is the starting point that will birth the other needed lifestyle habits that all work together to ensure great health. Naturally you must breathe, eat, and exercise properly to sustain a healthy life. However, if you do not think the proper thoughts about healthy living, you are already defeated long before you even get started.

> *A good man out of the good treasure of his heart brings forth good; and an evil man out of the evil treasure of his heart brings forth evil. For out of the abundance of the heart his mouth speaks* (Luke 6:45).

Your words are embryos that are birthed by your thoughts. Whatever your heart abundantly thinks about, that is what you will begin to say. Consider a baby who is just beginning to learn how to talk. Does he or she pick up an Oxford English Dictionary and immediately start reading all the words necessary in life? No, that is silly.

They hear words from adults and other older children around them on such a regular basis that their baby hearts soon fill up with words. At the appointed time babies start speaking the words that they understand. They choose the words that will cause others to immediately tend to their needs. Babies don't ask questions like, "How much is your net worth?" or "What time is the next private showing of the latest movie release?"

They ask only the questions that will yield them the results they are looking for. They say what they want. Because their English skills are limited and somewhat broken and because they have not been trained and developed in the art of communication, they use simple one-word commands like *bottle, eat, stop, sleep, mine, candy,* and their favorite word, *no.* These one-word commands get them results because everyone knows that when they speak, it is coming from the heart.

The Total Package

Babies are not usually pretentious. What they say is usually what they mean. Why? It comes from the abundance of their heart. In the same way, what comes from the abundance of your heart will be rewarded. This is precisely why you must be careful about what goes in your heart. The old adage says, "What goes in will inevitably come out." You speak what is in your heart. And what you speak becomes life or death to you.

Death and life are in the power of the tongue, and those who love it will eat its fruit (Proverbs 18:21).

You must be careful concerning what you say. Often, I hear misinformed people say things like, "I know I'm going die," or "I'll never get well; I'll always be sick." They repeat the negative report that their physician gives them concerning their health. But wouldn't it make better sense to pray against your bad diagnosis hoping that your prognosis will lead you to a sure cure? I would think so. However, most people say what they think.

You have the power to think thoughts that will produce words, that will in turn produce the character that is so needed to walk in divine health. Most disease and sickness worsen under the heavy load of stress and negativism. Hearing and saying words that are diametrically opposed to good health only invalidates the healing process. I cannot emphasize this point enough—you are what you say you are. In addition to that, you have what you say you have. You can be whatever you believe and say you can become.

Pleasant words are like a honeycomb, sweetness to the soul and health to the bones (Proverbs 16:24).

In this verse, the word *pleasant* literally means agreeableness. However, you don't have to agree with everybody's words. There are some things that you ought to disagree with when it's concerning your health. You have the right to cast down any word that is contrary to the power, purpose, and knowledge of God.

> *Casting down imaginations, and every high thing that exalteth itself against the knowledge of God, and bringing into captivity every thought to the obedience of Christ* (2 Corinthians 10:5 KJV).

Any words that don't support the concept of being totally healthy should sound very strange to your hearing. I have relatives who assure me that "everybody has to get sick." They tell me that "sickness is a natural part of life." They say, "You ought to expect it and plan for it." Most people have accepted this foolishness as truth.

"...you are what you say you are... you have what you say you have."

Saying those things are as foolish as saying, "Everybody has to go through foreclosure and repossession at some time. It's just inevitable." Doesn't that sound a bit ridiculous? For me it sounds equally ridiculous when I hear people trying to convince me that divine healing is a fantasy. The only reason why it is not your reality is because you don't think that it is possible for you.

When I am asked, "How are you?" or "How are you feeling today?" I always respond in the affirmative. I tell them, "I am well, I am wonderful, I am moving forward, I am getting better, and I am better than I was yesterday." I never give anyone the opportunity to join with me in pronouncing doom, death, and destruction on my own life. That negative spirit is powerful. You ask, "Well, isn't that being untruthful if you are not really feeling well?" No, it is not.

If someone who has a credible reputation pledges to send you a sizeable amount of money, you can go ahead and make plans based on that promise of money. You know in your heart that the money is on the way. Although you do not actually have the money in your hand, you are not worried because you know that it will be sent. Likewise, you don't have to worry about your health because God, with His credible reputation, has promised you good health. It may not look good right now, but good health is on the way.

How do you feel? The better question is, how do you want to feel? The answer to that question should determine your truest thoughts and ultimately the words that flow from those thoughts. You can work out on fitness equipment every day, eat the proper food choices, and drink plenty of water and yet still remain sick. Your health won't change until you change the way you *think* about your health. Remember the change that you really need comes from within, not from without.

Endnotes

1. William D. Danko and Thomas J. Stanley, *The Millionaire Next Door: Surprising Secrets of America's Wealthy* (New York: Pocket Books, a division of Simon and Schuster, 1996), 33-34.

Chapter Five

The Courage to Change

One of the things that is necessary to make you a better *you* is your willingness to change. Change is the only constant thing in life. Just think about it for a moment—everything in life changes. Nothing in life (other than God) remains the same. Although God never changes, our relationship toward Him changes as we come into a more mature and developing understanding and bond with Him.

If a baby remained the same size from the time he was born until he was 18 years of age, something would be drastically wrong. Suppose a child spoke the same way at 16 years old as he did at two years old. Most people would consider the child strange. In fact, we would label him as having some type of mental challenge. Why is that? It's because we expect people to change. If they don't then there has to be a problem.

The varied styles in the clothing of the 50's, 60's, 70's, and 80's are totally different than our more modern styles of dress. I realize there are certain clothing styles that have come back into circulation from previous eras, yet still only a small part of the mass population (usually teenagers) actually wears those styles now. Why is this? It's because change has to happen in order for people to go forward in life.

Change is necessary for growth in every area of your life. If a church does not grow, more than likely it is because in some area they refuse to change. If a business continues to report losses on their quarterlies, then that business has to make the necessary changes to bring the company out of the red. If a marriage is on the brink of divorce, then one of the parties must make the necessary adjustments in order to save the relationship.

"Change is necessary for growth in every area of your life."

It seems as if change is the solution to most problems. If change is so vital, then why don't more people just change? The reason why people refuse to change is because they have become comfortable with where they are now. They are comfortable with the status quo. If everybody in society is getting into debt with high-interest credit cards and loans, it won't seem abnormal for you to follow their bad example.

Human nature tends to gravitate toward the pathway of least resistance. "Whatever feels good" has been the motto for many Americans. Those good feelings come not because the situation is always a good one but rather because it has become a comfort zone. So for most folks, change is a mathematical equation to be avoided. Change = Massive Pain. Most people will do anything in their power to avoid pain. It hurts.

But truly, what really hurts is what most people have become so accustomed to—unfathomable debt, chronic illnesses, premature death, poverty and lack, and the belief that you will never live life at the 100-percent mark the way God intended you to live. That should be enormous pain. Since most people don't like to change, we have to give you reasons to change.

The Courage to Change

As I mentioned earlier, Ken the drywall man did not want to change his smoking habit when I first mentioned it to him. He opposed my suggestions and even made jokes about my commitment to health and healing. But now, since he is faced with a life-and-death dilemma, he is willingly choosing to change nearly everything in his life. He even changed from working as a self-employed individual to accepting disability checks from the state. He changed. My problem is that Ken did not change because he had a real choice in the matter. He changed because if he did not, he would be dead. To me that's kind of stupid.

Why should you wait until it's a life-and-death matter? Why should you make changes after you've lost everything? There are some choices that you have to make about whether or not you really want to be debt free, build wealth, grow rich, and be healthy, whole, and strong. You have to decide that in many areas of your life you will have to change. Your amount of savings will have to change if you are having a difficult time saving money each week. If you don't invest, you will have to start investing. If you are eating everything in your house and everybody else's house except the kitchen sink, you will have to change your eating habits. You will have to learn to avoid the three F's in food: fast food, fried food, and free food. All three are usually unhealthy.

If you are a junk food junkie you will have to change. No more chocolate bars until you get your health under control. And even then, you must limit your intake. If you are a diabetic, you have to change. I don't care how much insulin you have readily available, you have got to take all sugar and sugar-filled products out of your eating plan. If you don't change, you will die.

If you have high blood pressure, hypertension, gout, or digestion problems, then you need to remove red meats, including all pork products and beef, from your eating plan. You will need to replace much of what you eat with more vegetables, soy, tofu, fruits, and juiced products. You might say, "Those products taste horrible." Perhaps they taste that way to you now. But after you have made the change, you will become more and more accustomed to healthy foods, or as I call them, real foods. The reason they taste so strange to you is because you are not accustomed to eating them. As odd as this may sound, if you had started chewing on automobile tires when you were a child, by the time you reached adulthood you would have become accustomed to the taste of tires. In fact you may have even developed a liking for the taste of a good old-fashioned Michelin tire.

If you are a shop-aholic, a spend-aholic, and charge card-aholic, you will need to change. You've got to stop the spending cycle. You must cut up your charge cards and close your accounts before someone else does. You have to see yourself as an addict in need of recovery. I compare charge cards to crack and cocaine. In fact, I call them plastic crack. While you are charging, you get high. When the bill comes, you get low and have to charge to get high all over again. No matter how you look at it, for many people using charge cards is an addiction. I'm telling you that you have to kick your charge card addiction. You have to change.

Most people justify their use of credit cards saying, "I don't make enough money." I always tell people to save at least 10 to 20 percent of their income. In other words, give away only 80 to 90 percent of your income. If you don't, your income will drop to 60 percent because of the debt you have incurred. This will happen because you live at your means (not below). When unexpected things happen, such as automobile repairs or other emergency incidents (and they will happen), you fall into a perpetual cycle of debt.

You can get used to anything if you have it long enough. That is what this book is about—getting you used to making the right daily choices that in time will reward you with enormous blessings. As with anything else, it will take courage. Only the strong survive;

only the courageous win and conquer uncharted territory. Are you strong? Are you one of the winners whose story we will hear about?

I believe you are. For starters, you are actually reading this book. It's obvious that you are not like the many illiterate or borderline illiterate people in society who refuse to read anything other than the funnies in the comic section of the newspaper. You are reading this because deep down within you, you really want to change. You want to see a major revolution in your finances.

You want to master money and not have money master you. You want to be in control of your health. The days of being sick and tired are over for you. Yes, you really do have the courage to change. But as you do, let me caution that you must also have the courage to stand against your enemies.

As strange as it may sound, for every step that you make toward success in life, there will always be a devil assigned to totally disrupt the process toward attaining your success. Don't allow yourself to get off track or be distracted by people who don't have the same desires as you do.

In fact, one of the greatest ways to make your necessary change is to surround yourself with people who have already done what you want to do or are on their way. Being in the company of the courageous will only strengthen and encourage your faith to do what God has commanded all His children to do—the impossible!

Be strong and of good courage, for to this people you shall divide as an inheritance the land which I swore to their fathers to give them. Only be strong and very courageous, that you may observe to do according to all the law which Moses My servant commanded you; do not turn from it to the right hand or to the left, that you may prosper wherever you go. This Book of the Law shall not depart from your mouth, but you shall meditate in it day and night, that you may observe to do according to all that is written in it. For

The Total Package

then you will make your way prosperous, and then you will have good success (Joshua 1:6-8).

Chapter Six

What Is Today's Forecast?

Most everyone has heard a local meteorologist report his or her prediction about whether it is going to be sunny, cloudy, rainy, icy, or blizzard conditions. Within a two or three-day period the skilled weather person can usually nail down what kind of day to expect. But when trying to forecast the weather over a long term, most weathermen are very inaccurate in their predictions.

The reason they inaccurately forecast the weather is because some things are left for God alone to decide upon. Only God really knows what the weather is going to be like. Even when we think that we have a sure handle on it, God will change His course of action. Although many have tried to, we cannot pin God down for He is Sovereign.

But when predicting the outlook of your financial future and your health, you really don't have to leave much to chance. God's Word is heavily loaded with Scriptures that support both your health and wealth. What about your overall future? Does God really have good thoughts about your future? The concept that many people have about God can be somewhat confusing and is most of the time very inaccurate.

"...money is a magnifier. It doesn't corrupt character; it magnifies it."

Some people believe that God wants people to suffer from financial ruin. I've heard people say, "God does not want people to have wealth. People would be much better off if they had less." I think that statement is more a matter of opinion than actual truth. I know for certain that if you have more, you can do more to be a blessing to people. Remember what we said earlier, money is a magnifier. It doesn't corrupt character; it magnifies it.

Put money in the hands of Billy Graham or Oral Roberts and they will use it to get the world saved, healed, and delivered in the name of Jesus. Put money in the hands of Pastor Tommy Barnett, pastor of the Phoenix First Assembly of God, and he will purchase more school buses and passenger vans in order to transport people to church. Put money in the hands of Oprah Winfrey and she is bound to give it to her favorite charity. Children Evangelist Bill Wilson will use money to help children victimized by life in the streets of Brooklyn, New York. It's what you do with money that really counts.

Others ignorantly believe that God wants people to get sick and die prematurely. For the most part, people live life waiting for the next tragedy to happen. In fact, most people are afraid to live life to the fullest. They think that if a whole lot of good things happen to them, then bad things are inevitably around the corner. What a sad scenario. The real truth is that God has great plans for you. That's your forecast.

Today's Forecast

For I know the thoughts that I think toward you, says the Lord, thoughts of peace and not of evil, to give you a future and a hope (Jeremiah 29:11).

According to the Word of God, your prognosis is promising. God has thoughts of peace and prosperity toward you, not evil intentions. Although your checkbook may not agree and although your last checkup with the doctor may say differently, you have hope. If you have made it this far in the book, keep on reading because your chances of acquiring the total package increases greatly with each word that you read, understand, and act on.

In Part 3, we will show you how to get out of debt, how to eat to live, and how to design an exercise plan that is best for you. We will show you what investments to avoid and which ones are best for you in the present market. We also will help you understand why God wants you to be healthy and wealthy.

There is an anti-prosperity cult on the rise in America. They preach a false gospel of poverty and sickness. Unfortunately, they are very productive because Satan knows well that if the Church of Jesus Christ becomes impoverished, as these false preachers encourage them to be, then the gospel message of the Kingdom will never reach the world. According to the Scriptures, not preaching this kingdom message will only delay the coming of the Lord.

> *And this gospel of the kingdom shall be preached in all the world for a witness unto all nations; and then shall the end come* (Matthew 24:14 KJV).

This delay will then give Satan more time to cause more evil and destruction. So it is imperative that the Body of Christ at large seizes the wealth needed to make the impact on the world that God desires us to make.

Although I thoroughly believe that the cross represents for many Christians, including myself, a symbol of great suffering, it does have an even greater meaning. Every believer should expect to endure suffering as a good solider, just as the cross on one hand represents suffering. But on the other side of the cross (about three days later), we (the believers) share in Christ's victory. Consequently, no one suffers for the sake of the gospel in this life without also experiencing great victory. We don't suffer just to suffer. We don't go through trials without the hopes of coming out on top. We endure pain with purpose.

> So Jesus answered and said, "Assuredly, I say to you, there is no one who has left house or brothers or sisters or father or mother or wife or children or lands, for My sake and the gospel's, who shall not receive a hundredfold now in this time—houses and brothers and sisters and mothers and children and lands, with persecutions—and in the age to come, eternal life. But many who are first will be last, and the last first" (Mark 10:29-31).

Concerning finances some have been born into families who have never exercised any financial reasoning. These children started out with a clear disadvantage in comparison to those who were born into wealth. Others have ignorantly made and continue to make horrible financial choices and subsequently feel the consequences every single day. Then there is a small minority group of people who have been born into wealth and taught the principles of the wealthy from the time they were small.

All of the Lewis children have been born into a health legacy that began with their father—me, Pastor Aaron. From the time my children were born, they have been indoctrinated with my healthy eating teachings. So now, eating the proper foods is a natural part of their lives, not drudgery. Because they are still children and are often exposed to other people in school and various family members who don't embrace my philosophies on healthy living, they may occasionally stray. But by and large, they don't wander too far because they were born hearing, "Thus saith..." concerning their eating habits. In one respect they were born with a great-looking forecast for their health.

I realize that people are not born knowing how to live and walk in divine health. As with anything else, it must be taught. Although this book is not the end-all to health and wealth, it is a more than complete package to launch you far past your expectations for yourself. So whether you were born into a family who provided you with the knowledge or not, it does not matter. In the next section we will help to bring you up to snuff. No longer will you have to feel disadvantaged. We will give you the information that, once used, will provide you too with the winner's edge. Get excited, for your future looks great!

The Total Package

Part 3

The Cure

"A healing or being healed; restoration to health or a sound condition."

Chapter Seven

The Process Toward Possession

Then Joshua said to the children of Israel: "How long will you neglect to go and possess the land which the Lord God of your fathers has given you?" (Joshua 18:3)

*So they said, "Arise, let us go up against them. For we have **seen** the land, and indeed it is very good. Would you do nothing? Do not hesitate to go, and enter to possess the land. When you go, you will come to a secure people and a large land. For God has given it into your hands, a place where there is no lack of anything that is on the earth"* (Judges 18:9-10, emphasis added).

How Long Will You Wait?

Just as it was in biblical times, so is the human tendency now to be afraid, or to outright procrastinate when it comes to possessing the inheritance that God has given. Joshua asked the children of Israel, *"How long will you neglect to go and possess the land?"* The land was available and ready to be utilized by the people.

The Total Package

God gave it to them, yet they waited. The words "*how long*" reveal that financial blessing has a time limit on it. It has an expiration date. It will not wait for you to get ready. You've got to already be in place to receive your blessing. If you won't seize it, someone else surely will.

During the late 60's up until the late 70's there was a tremendous door of opportunity open for African-Americans to purchase homes. This privilege was not as readily available to them prior to the passing of the Civil Rights Bill. But when this door of opportunity finally opened, it offered affordable housing to industrial working-class citizens, through loan programs that were tailor-made to fit their individual budgets.

Single homes and two and three-family houses sold for less than $15,000. In most cases the expected down payment was five percent or less. The federal government in conjunction with major lending institutions worked collaboratively to get as many people of color into houses as possible. The way was made easy. This window of opportunity was open on and off for about ten years, then it closed.

After that period, African-Americans could still purchase homes, but the criteria (credit rating and the amount of money needed for the down payment) became a bit more stringent. When this window had been wide open, thousands of black people went right through it. There were, on the other hand, thousands of black people who decided that they would wait until the time was right in their minds to make the move.

To this day I cannot understand exactly what they were waiting for. I'm not sure why they waited so long to make the move toward buying a home. This was a time when poor credit and lack of a substantial down payment were being waived as contingency factors. On top of that, what they would have paid for their mortgage would have been far less than their rent payments.

The Process Toward Possession

Now more than 30 years later, thousands of these same people have not yet purchased a home. They are still renting and making their landlords richer, not to mention that they are still complaining and bellyaching about how they can't get ahead in life. Why is this? Why did some seize the opportunity and others choose not to?

I'm not sure I can answer that question for all of them. Perhaps they were scared to make the move. Fear is truly an immobilizing spirit whose roots are demonic. Maybe they had been renters for so long that renting was the only concept they could envision for themselves. They had become accustomed to living their lives in the comfort zone of lack and complacency.

In the late 90's the stock market was roaring and people were saying, "Stocks are too high. Let me know when they come down." Now the stock market is lower than it has been in quite some time and their excuse is, "The market is too low," or "I'll wait until it goes back up." But the bottom line is that their inactivity is causing them to lose more money than they would have lost if they had just invested.

Because of fear many folks took all their money out of the stock market and began to invest in real estate. Although real estate is a great investment, the problem is that current real estate prices are at an all-time high. Many people are selling their stocks at seventy to sixty cents on the dollar and buying real estate for $1.20, and they think they are getting ahead. But most people are purchasing property far beyond the market's real value. I did not say comparable or sales value. I said real value. The real value is what your house will be worth when the housing market begins to fall.

When the real estate market crashes, people who have invested all their money in real estate will be crying because they used bad timing judgment in making their decision. When the real estate market is high, often stocks are low. When stocks are high, often houses are more affordable than ever. It's just a cycle. It's just the way it is. Whichever market is favorable, you ought to do something and not be totally inactive.

Are You Afraid to Fly?

I once heard a story about an eagle that somehow had broken its leg and as a result needed medical attention. The eagle was taken out of its natural habitat and confined for several months to a cage where it could be observed and treated as its leg slowly healed. The day finally came when the bird's leg was completely healed and it was time for it to be released back into its habitat.

The bird was carried out to a mountain to be set free. Everyone knew for sure that this bird would be so happy to get back out into its natural surroundings. But to their total surprise, when they opened the door of the cage, they noticed that this bird did not make any advances to fly away. In fact, it lay down and acted as if it did not want to leave. After hours went by, the veterinarians determined that they would have to literally force this eagle out of the cage and make it fly again.

What happened to the eagle? The eagle had become so accustomed to the cage and to the catering that it did not want to leave. It became afraid to fly. Although it was created to fly, its new environment had victimized this bird. Are you much like this eagle? God created you to rule. Are you ruling? If not, why aren't you? Do you frown at business opportunities, purchasing stock options, buying foreclosed properties, or jumping on the next great investment? If you do, then you are much like this eagle that became so comfortable doing nothing.

The problem is that these people had been offered a great real estate opportunity, but now it is gone. Within the past four decades this type of door opened three or four times to people of all ethnic backgrounds. Yet, there are still millions who are waiting for the supernatural to happen, not realizing that the supernatural is already happening. This is so unfortunate. You cannot possess what right-fully belongs to you if you are slothful.

He also that is slothful in his work is brother to him that is a great waster (Proverbs 18:9 KJV).

Using What You Already Have

I've heard people say so many times, "I wish I had a million dollars. If I only had a million dollars, I wouldn't have any financial problems." That statement is empty and untruthful. If you have financial problems with the money you have now, you'll proba-bly have greater financial problems with more. Think about it: If you worked a job for 25 years and made an average of $40,000 each year over that period of time, you have already earned one million dollars in gross wages.

"If you have financial problems with the money you have now, you'll probably have greater financial problems with more."

So the question should not be whether a million dollars will come through your hands or not. The question should be, what are you going to do with the million dollars once it comes? Everybody has money. In fact, you really don't need any more investment money than you already have in your possession right now to get started. You have to use what you already have as a power-filled seed to get started.

If you are working for someone else or if you are self-employed, you get paid on some type of regular basis. You might get paid once each week, once every two weeks, or each time you complete a job you are hired to do. However you get paid, you are responsible to prove to God and yourself with each check that you deserve to get an increase.

The Total Package

Many Christians are notorious for complaining about why they don't have the wealth that they think they deserve. They are searching for wealth, but they already have it. The wealth that you need to acquire greater wealth is already in your hands; *you already have it.* So why are you still in lack? Why aren't you living as financially well as you would like to live?

Consider the "Jesus Financial Principle": "Because you have been faithful over a few things, I will make you ruler over many things. Enter into the joy of your Lord."

If you are not faithful with a little, why would God give you more? If you are not a faithful steward with $100 a week income, why would God give you $1000 or $10,000 a week to misappropriate? God is not an idiot. He has plenty of worthwhile things that He wants to do with money in this earthly realm. If you are not faithful in increasing your wealth on a small level, then you will never increase on a larger scale.

Most young teenagers are not faithful with money. Hence, their parents do not give them much money. For example, you can give a teenager $170 to go school shopping. After a full day of shopping, many teenagers will return home, not with a bag full of clothes and supplies, but with just one pair of sneakers.

With great pride they will spend $170 on one pair of sneakers and think nothing of it, not considering that it was a bad choice to invest in. If you were that child's parent would you be inclined to give him or her more money? Of course you wouldn't. After discovering that your child did not know how to handle money properly, you would decide not to give them more until they mastered how to appropriate what you had already given them.

Here's an extremely important question: How much of your dollars is being applied toward owning something? Remember that's what this book is all about—getting you to become financially free through ownership. If you are leasing a car and renting a house, don't even bother answering the question. You are at ground zero.

The Process Toward Possession

Your truthful answer to this question will determine whether you are faithful or not in a few things.

You ask, "How can my money go towards owning something each week? Does that mean that I have to make a purchase on a weekly basis?" You are absolutely correct. Just like you purchase groceries each week, pay your bills each month, and create unnecessary debts each day, you should be investing or spending your money on things that you can own.

Remember to always consciously purchase things that will appreciate in value over a period of time. Clothes don't appreciate in value, unless Elvis Presley previously owned them and you sold it to Christie's in New York. Sorry, if you are buying clothes for yourself, they aren't going to increase in value. Going out to eat, in most cases, is a loss, particularly if you are trying to build wealth.

There is nothing wrong with going out every now and then. It is when it becomes a habit that you will notice financial decrease. If you are going out to spend relational time together, you should instead choose to rent a movie and cook your own food. It's a lot cheaper, more intimate, and makes better financial sense. So clothes, food, movie tickets, and theme park passes are all fun to buy, but they will eventually work against your wealth building plan. Buy things that you can own, that have some real value. Following are some suggestions of things you can invest your money into that have the potential to give you a return.

You can own:

1. Real estate—commercial buildings, residential property.

2. Raw land.

3. Stocks.

4. Mutual funds.

5. An automobile (that's paid for).

6. A business.

7. Intellectual property ("authorship"—books, songs, software).

8. Having cash at your disposal.

9. Gold and silver.

10. Anything that once purchased has the capacity to appreciate in value.

Every time you get paid you ought to somehow invest into one or more of these areas. If you are paying on your mortgage, you are increasing your net worth and your assets with each payment. Stocks go up and down. But when they go up, they really go up. Don't squander in the area of automobile spending. Cars are rolling stock and they do depreciate. However, most cars that are kept in good condition will have some cash value. It is not a good idea to lease a car unless it is a business expense. Then it can be used as a tax write-off.

"Use your money to create prosperity."

Buy a business. Invest in an already existing network marketing business. Write a song or a book or create a software package. This is intellectual property that will earn a residual income for as long as your product is selling. Gold and silver have been known to keep its face value all the time. In fact, both gold and silver keep their value even in volatile markets.

If you use your money to *own* something, then you are proving yourself faithful before God. When you do so, God will cause great wealth to overtake you because He knows that you can be trusted. Be warned that one sure way to stop the natural and supernatural flow of wealth from coming into your life is to simply do nothing with what you already have.

Use your money to create prosperity. In fact, the term for your money throughout the remaining chapters will be "prosperity dollars."

The Process Toward Possession

Prosperity dollars is money, that when used, will cause more money to come back to you. If you give money to support a person's drug habit then your prosperity dollars will turn into cursed dollars. If you use your money to buy your boyfriend food, clothing, and shelter because he is too lazy to do it himself, that money is money lost.

Prosperity Dollars Investment Chart: I Will Give/Sow Into...

To God, His Church and His People	To My Family and Myself	To My Future
Tithing (10% of my income)	Investments	Education
Generous Offerings	401K, 403B, IRA	College, University
Missions	Real Estate	Continuing Education
Almsgiving	Stocks	Workshops & Seminars

Possessing the Sinners' Wealth

A good man leaveth an inheritance to his children's children: and the wealth of the sinner is laid up for the just (Proverbs 13:22 KJV).

A favorite Scripture for many Christians in these perplexing times is Proverbs 13:22. Many Christians would love to get their hands on the wealth that all rich sinners now enjoy. I've seen and heard Christians run down the aisles of church screaming at the top of their lungs, confessing that the wealth of the sinner is laid up for the righteous. But that's the only thing they do. Somehow they believe that just by screaming and spitting, and spurting out a tongue or two, God is going to transfer the enormous amount of wealth that is in the hands of sinners to them.

The Total Package

I really hate to be the one to bear sad news, but God is not going to do such a thing. If the wealth that you desire is in the hands of the sinner, how do you think you are going to get it? And if they are sinners, I am sure they won't have any problem doing every sinful thing within their power to stop you from getting their money. You can't just go up to a tycoon and say, "Thus says the Lord of Israel, let my money go." It doesn't work like that. The transference of wealth to the Body of Christ will not be given to financially illiterate believers.

The wealth transfer will be delivered into the hands of believers who have taken the time and worked hard to educate themselves about money. The ones who have learned how money works and the laws that govern investing are the likely candidates to receive the great transference. Be honest with yourself. Do you really believe that you are qualified to handle millions, possibly billions, of dollars right now when you can barely balance your checkbook?

Do you pay your utilities, your credit card bills, and your mortgage or rents on time all of the time? If you don't, then you are not the one to receive the great wealth transfer. I am not saying that God won't bless you beyond where you are now. He will. But I am saying that He's probably not going to give you billions of dollars to waste on foolish and irresponsible spending choices. He's going to set the person up with major bucks who intuitively knows how to turn whatever God gives him into far more—all for His glory and His Kingdom.

The good man who leaves an inheritance for his children's children obviously understands how a trust actually works. And this good man was able throughout the course of his lifetime to pass on the knowledge to his children who in turn will educate their children about the same principles of wealth transfer and estate planning.

Understanding trusts can be a somewhat complicated subject. Not only does it require great understanding but it also requires an ongoing education because laws change continually. Wealth will only go into the hands of the righteous who understand what to do with the wealth once it comes.

The next time you hear "the wealth of the sinner is laid up for the righteous," instead of getting overly excited, get prepared. Ask God to make you eligible to receive the wealth. Go to your local community college and take some financial investment and financial management classes. Buy books like the one you are reading now about wealth and health. Regularly listen to tapes on the subject. Go to moneymaking seminars and financial investment seminars. Learn as much as you possibly can.

The qualifications for the wealth transfer are twofold. The first part most Christians have already received by God's grace—salvation. However, all Christians will have to receive the second part through study and application—financial literacy. You have to know and comprehend the language of wealth. Then and only then will you be qualified to become excited when you hear about the great wealth transfer. Remember that it takes both parts, not just one.

The Total Package

Chapter Eight

Growing Rich

When I travel to conduct seminars around the country I often stay at a hotel that is located in the downtown area of a city. And I can't help but to notice from my hotel room, the many superstructures. More likely than not, insurance companies or banks occupy the largest buildings in the city. Have you ever wondered why companies such as banks and insurance companies own the largest, most elaborate buildings?

They are the businesses making most of the money, and subsequently, are able to afford buildings with marble flooring, oriental carpeting, and high skywalks. If you want to be rich, you might want to take note of these types of companies, because you have to follow the example of the rich. You have to do exactly what they do in order to accomplish the same results that they accomplish. Conversely, you should avoid doing the things that they don't do.

How Do the Rich Make Their Money?

If I gave you $7.00 for every $1.00 you gave me, how long would you keep giving me your $1.00 in exchange for my $7.00?

The Total Package

You would probably give it to me indefinitely. How about if I gave you $18.00 or $24.00 in exchange for every $1.00 that you gave to me, how long would you let me give you my money? I already know the answer. Well, simply put, that is how the rich make their money. Someone like you gives the rich folks $7.00, $18.00, $24.99, and they give you, in return, a fresh crisp one-dollar bill. The amazing thing is that you continue to do this indefinitely and with a smile.

The rich don't do what the poor do. For the most part, folks who are broke usually put all their money in the bank. The rich don't do this. They want to have total control of their money all the time. They want to know that their money is working for them. The rich use the bank only for the purpose of paying monthly bills and expenses.

They don't put twenty and thirty thousand dollars into the bank to watch it sit and do nothing. They put only enough money in the bank to cover their monthly budget and no more. They won't put large sums of money in the bank because they know that they lose money by putting it in a conventional savings account. In my area the average interest paid on a regular savings account is from 0.75 to 1 percent.

That means you will earn about $1.00 each year for investing your $100 with them. At that interest rate, it will take eons before you ever become wealthy. How about most CDs? Most banks will pay you no more than three percent on a CD, which means at the end of the year you have earned a whopping $3.00. But think again.

If inflation is at 3.5 percent, which is about average, then you are back at $100. I'm not finished yet. You will then be charged federal taxes (about 28 percent) and state taxes (about 7 percent) on your money. Now you are at a loss, somewhere around $97.00. I've not even included the amount that you will lose if you decide to take your money out sooner. The penalty totally invalidates your investment. This just does not make good financial sense.

In addition, most people get direct deposit, which means you lose immediate control over what happens with your money. The other day I noticed an advertisement in the bank promising that if you opened a checking account with direct deposit, you would receive a brand-new portable compact disc player. What an enticement. A corresponding flyer listed the incentives for opening up the account: Easy to do, Saves time, Convenient, Secure, Reliable, and Fast. The only thing that it forgot to list is that when you do open an account, you give the power of control of your funds to the bank, which then makes billions of dollars in revenue for them. They didn't mention that, so I thought I would.

What happens when you give them your money either through direct deposit or a 0.75-percent interest savings account? Check it out.

When You Give the Bank Your Money for:	The Bank Gives You:	They Lend Your Money at:
Savings	1% — (*note these are high figures)	4.9%—9 % for a home mortgage
a CD	3% — (*note these are high figures)	9%—14.99 for an automobile loan
a Money Market Account	Relative	13.99%—24.99% for a credit card
an Interest Bearing Checking Account	Relative	11.5%—19.99% for a personal unsecured loan

The Total Package

When the bank lends your money at up to 25 percent more than they are paying you, no wonder they get richer and you get poorer. Basically, you are giving them your $25.00 for their dollar bill. It is impossible to get ahead like this. The rich are on the opposite end of this lopsided equation. They are the lenders, not the borrowers. These examples epitomize the Scripture in Proverbs 22:7 that says, *"The rich rules over the poor, and the borrower is servant to the lender."*

Unfortunately, until you get on the other side of the coin, the rich will always rule over you. Instead of lending your money to the banks, why not buy Fannie Mae, Freddie Mac (government secured loans sold in bundles of 100 backed by the FDIC), or Sallie Mae (government student loans) that have defaulted? There are always bad loans. There are always people who can't pay their debts. If you invest into bad debts that are federally backed, your interest-bearing power will increase dramatically. Instead of earning a mere one percent, you can earn from seven to ten percent.

Most wealthy people invest in bonds, stocks, and real estate. Some also invest in tax liens. There are homeowners all across America who struggle to pay the taxes on their homes. If the taxes remain unpaid, the town or city that they owe the taxes to will eventually take the house away. You can buy a tax lien, which means that you pay off the taxes on the home, which helps to save their property and you lien their house at an interest rate of 12 to 20 percent each year. If they pay the interest you win, and if they don't pay at all, you still win because you will have a house worth far more in value than your initial investment.

Of all the rich folks I know, there are three distinguishable factors that all seem to have in common.

1. They own or are the heads of extremely profitable businesses. Most did not inherit their wealth.

100

2. They have invested the money from their profits. They usually invest 10 to 20 percent of their profits over a long period of time. They are patient and tend to hold their stocks, real estate, and other investments for a long time.

3. They are disciplined. They will do whatever it takes to make it work.

Oh, Mr. and Mrs. Consumer

It is very important for you to become more stock conscious and less consuming conscious. What I mean is that if you own stock interest in a corporation that markets your favorite products, you can help increase your own net worth every time you purchase those products. What sense does it make to buy tons of toothpaste, soap, perfumes, clothing, sneakers, computer-related products, groceries, and automobiles, but not own stock with any of those companies?

The rich own stock in companies and buy products connected with those same companies. Although Pastor Aaron is totally healthy, he has one nutritional flaw—he's addicted to Skittles candies. Skittles are probably the only candy that you will regularly catch Pastor Aaron cheating with. Other than Skittles, he lives "by the book." Skittles is a product of the M&M/Mars Corporation. It would make wonderful sense for him to purchase stock in the M&M/Mars Corporation. I am not recommending that this stock is a choice stock. I am merely suggesting that you invest in what you are already consuming.

You should buy only the stock you believe in and hopefully use. Every time you use your products, you get richer. Every time you use their products, they get richer. Whoever owns the stock earns the dividends. If you love NIKE, Reebok, or ADIDAS sneakers, then consider buying their stock. There are thousands of companies that are publicly traded, far too many for me to list. My point is, if you are already using the product and you have a sense of product loyalty, why not get more deeply involved in the money-making process?

Three Things You Need to Do to Start Investing Now

1. Find a financial advisor with a variety of services and payment plans. If a financial advisor knows only how to handle insurance policies, that is the only type of investment he or she will offer you: insurance. If they are limited, you will be also. You need to find someone who works with a myriad of different kinds of investments from mutual funds to stocks to bonds to insurance. Interview at least three different advisors to see which one is best for you. Ask them what kind of clients they are accustomed to dealing with. If they deal only with people who have at least $100,000 to invest, then you might not receive their undivided attention if you are investing $5,000. You want an advisor who is used to handling clients just like you. So ask questions.

2. Begin to build a complete financial plan. You need to have several things building at the same time, not just one. You should diversify your investments. You should be building a mutual fund—retirement fund—college fund—long-term care policy—change of lifestyle fund. Some of my clients ask me to invest in the one big investment that will make them rich. If I knew the answer to that, I would be richer and famous. Many people think that wealth building is like hitting the lottery. It is not. Wealth building takes time and concentrated effort. It's when you work all your "irons" together that one or even many will produce the results that you intended in time. *"Cast your bread upon the*

102

waters, for after many days you will find it again" (Eccl. 11:1 NIV).

3. Execute your plan. You must deposit money into your fund on a consistent basis. Don't procrastinate and put off until tomorrow. You've heard it said before, "Tomorrow is not promised to you." Don't put off until tomorrow the things that you should be doing today. Most people want to be wealthy but few are disciplined enough to see their wealth come to fruition.

Real estate is probably one of the most profitable ways that the rich get rich. Unlike stocks, which you have to purchase with money, you can literally buy real estate without having to use any of your money if you qualify for no-money-down financing programs. Real estate value increases and tends to hold its value over a period of time. There are wonderful books on the subject of real estate investing.

Write to us and we will be glad to send you a list of books that we personally recommend. If you want to understand the language of the rich, and stocks, bonds, and mutual funds, you need to order *Millionaires in Training: The Wealth Builder* by George B. Thompson. This great resource will further your knowledge about the wonderful world of the stock market.

The Total Package

Chapter Nine

Getting Out of Debt

In order to live the wealthy life that God intended for you to live, you need to understand that debt cannot be a lifestyle for you. You have to do everything in your natural power to get out of debt forever. This chapter is dedicated to giving you debt elimination strategies that work. Whether you have acquired two million dollars worth of debt or two hundred dollars, the same strategies will work if applied.

Understand that debt is debt. However, I want you to understand that there are many levels of debt and different kinds of debtors. The person who earns billions of dollars acquires a different kind of debt than the person who earns $25,000 annually. When you owe multiple millions of dollars worth of debt, your creditor handles you a bit differently than if you owe money for a car or a four-bedroom house both valued under $200,000.

If you owe twenty million dollars in real estate debt, your creditor will be more likely to come to an understandable agreement than if your house goes into foreclosure. Some creditors have extended so much credit that it would not be worthwhile for them to repossess or foreclose on property because they would never recoup their loss-es. Consequently, they would rather come to an agreement than to readily accept such a tremendous loss.

So am I saying that your goal should be to amass enormous amounts of debt so that your debt will be in a safe zone? No, that is not what I am saying at all. I believe what the Scripture says about debt. *"Owe no one anything except to love one another, for he who loves another has fulfilled the law"* (Rom. 13:8). This Scripture doesn't say that it is a sin to get a loan, as some people may think. Let's be honest and real. Most people in this country, even the rich, would be poor to this very day if it were not for the ability to borrow within reason.

Borrowing can be a blessing, particularly if you borrow to buy something that has real value or appreciating value. Banks are not demons, so stop being paranoid. It's not a sin to get a car loan or a house mortgage. For most folks it's the only way you will ever own a home or an automobile. So don't let anyone make you feel bad because you borrowed money that was needed. What message then is Romans 13:8 trying to convey? This Scripture says that the only debt you will never be able to pay off is the debt of LOVE.

No matter how long you live or how much you have loved, you will always be obligated to love one another. You will always be indebted to the law of love because that law can never be paid in full, which brings to mind the message that every other debt should be paid off in a timely fashion. If your other debts cannot be paid off within an appro-priate amount of time, it's probably a debt that you should not have.

For example, credit cards that hold high-debt balances are rarely paid off. In the rare times that they are paid off, they are quickly used to charge high amounts all over again. Usually they carry balances forever and ever, amen. It appears that credit cards can be listed as a debt that is never paid off. Like the Energizer bunny, your debt keeps going and growing until it has turned into a big ugly monster that you can't even recognize. For the most part your credit card debts are greed debts, not necessary ones. We have to deal with your credit card debts upfront.

However, at times, credit cards do serve a purpose. For example, our travel system has made it extremely convenient to book airline tickets and hotel rooms as well as rent automobiles with a major credit card. If you don't have a major credit card, it can be difficult for you to travel to the next city or country. For the purposes of travel you should have a credit card.

Also, for the purpose of emergencies you should have a major credit card. You never know when a loved one may die or another emergency will arise. In those cases a credit card comes in very handy. Other than those times, you should not use your credit card at all. If you have had a problem in the past being totally undisciplined with your credit card, then you need to consider not using a credit card for a long time.

Avoid Debt Purchases

The other day I was reading the newspaper and ran across a "rent-a" type company that makes their profit by renting you inferior items at an overly inflated price. They advertised a lacquer-laminated, low-quality bedroom set for $17.99 each week. At the end of the 104 weeks, they stated, you would have paid only $1,870.96. That wouldn't be so bad, except this bedroom set is worth only about $699 at best.

They also advertised an air conditioner that you could buy at Wal-Mart or Target for $95 to $109. Their so-called deal promoted the $25.99 special. After 30 weeks you will have paid only $779.70. And we can't forget the big-screen, Super Bowl television set special. After you finish paying for this 42-inch television, you will have paid only $3,982.33. What a deal! Or, what a dummy?

These debt purchases need to be avoided at all cost. If you really "need" them, put them on layaway if possible. At least you won't be charged an unfathomable amount of interest. And when you pick up the item that you've purchased, it will be paid in full. Don't even step into those businesses that rent anything. Think ownership. Most reputable furniture companies will set up a payment schedule (a type of layaway plan) for you if you simply ask them.

Interestingly enough, you will never find these rental gimmick stores in upscale communities. They are always located in areas where the people are poorer and less educated. They intentionally prey on those who are misinformed and those who just don't know any better. You will probably never see a "rent-a" type store in Beverly Hills, California; Greenwich, Connecticut; Princeton, New Jersey; or Boca Raton, Florida. But you will see them juxtaposed to ever major urban city in America. These stores are not a solution to your problem but a fiendish way to perpetuate your encumbering condition.

Using Your Mind

Naturally you will have to use your mind if you are going to get debt free and stay there. Consider many things that you purchased just last year—you can't even use them anymore. Why then did you get in debt because of them? You did not use your mind. You allowed your emotions to take the place of your mental logic and reasoning. From now on, you have always got to be in control. You have to use your M.I.N.D.

M–Money

> *For wisdom is a defense as money is a defense, but the excellence of knowledge is that wisdom gives life to those who have it* (Ecclesiastes 7:12).

Although people continually try to diminish the value of money, the Bible puts money in the same category as wisdom. Just as wisdom is a defense, so is money. You can use whatever amount of money you have right now as a defense against debt. With each paycheck you can drastically decrease your debt by applying small payments of what you already have in hand toward your debt over a long period of time. It's your consistency that is going to pay off in the long run. Be patient; your freedom is just around the corner.

"You can use whatever amount of money you have right now as a defense against debt."

I–Intelligence

You need to use your intelligence, financial discernment, and judgment when it comes to your money and decreasing your debts. Having to keep up with the Jones will keep you broke. Being in debt because you are fascinated with designer clothing is just not intelligent. Intelligence would provoke you to open up your own clothing line, creating an opportunity in which people start paying you money. Now that's intelligence! It is beyond unintelligence to buy your child $100 to $200 sneakers. I have a rule called the dunk rule. It states: If your child cannot dunk a basketball, then they do not need a $100 or $200 pair of sneakers. I see young misinformed mothers buying their infant babies brand-name sneakers costing $59.99 to $79.99. Not only can't these babies dunk a basketball, they can't even walk yet. You have to use far greater intelligence if you are *serious* about becoming debt free. For now, not always, you will have to pass up some things in life. You can't always go to the movies with your friends, go out to eat with buddies, and take your dream vacations. There will be times that you have to say, "No. I can't get the brand-new clothes I want because I am working for something better. I want to be out of debt. I can't get the new car now because I'm using my intelligence. That money could be far better used on decreasing my debt which inevitably will make me wealthier in the process."

109

The Total Package

N–Need

> *May He give you the desire of your heart and make all your plans succeed* (Psalm 20:4 NIV).

Succinctly put, your desire to be truly wealthy and debt free should be greater than your need to have temporary wants. The word *need* in this case can be replaced with the word *desire*. You may have a *need* to be seen, noticed, and recognized. Perhaps you believe you *need* to wear clothes or purchase items that give you an emotional charge. When using your M.I.N.D., your passion for purposeful wealth overrides all those things that tend to provide you with temporary satisfaction. You've got real desire, and real desire is always followed by actions and character that coincide with that desire. The next time you want to justify a purchase, say this: "I need to be debt free." Just keep saying that until you start believing and acting on the words you are saying. Imagine what life would be like if you did not have debts to pay. That should be enough motivation for you to change your confession about what you *think* you need to what you *actually* do need.

> *Desire is the germ of the mind.*
> *There is no creation without it.*[1]
> Zora Neale Hurston

D–Discipline

> *Go therefore and make disciples of all the nations, baptizing them in the name of the Father and of the Son and of the Holy Spirit, teaching them to observe all things that I have commanded you; and lo, I am with you always, even to the end of the age. Amen* (Matthew 28:19-20).

I know that people in our society love quick fixes. I will be honest with you—there are no quick fixes when it comes to getting out of debt. It's going to take hard work, determination, and *discipline*.

Discipline is the training that will birth the needed self-control in the areas of spending and investing. Without discipline you might as well close this book and not read any further. Discipline will not kill you; it will help you to achieve your goals in life. When you are not disciplined you make purchases that you cannot justify. Why would you purchase a pair of $125 basketball shoes for your child when he doesn't play basketball? That's like buying a $2000 crossbow yet never learning to shoot it. I've seen people buy professional BMX bicycles that cost more than $3000, but they never ride them.

"It's going to take hard work, determination, and discipline."

Just as you need discipline to spend properly, you also need discipline to save and invest. Every time you put a certain amount of money aside for savings or investing, your mind will play spending tricks on you—*"You could have bought this or that with your money."* Discipline, however, keeps the goal always in mind. Isn't it strange how a person can be grossly overweight yet continue to do the things and eat the things that caused them to gain weight in the first place? "I can't leave cake alone. I'll die for pork chops. I can't drink water, it has no taste; I'd rather drink colas." Lack of discipline will keep you fat and unhealthy. Lack of discipline will also get you and keep you broke. When Jesus gave the great commission He never said, "Go make converts." Yet this is exactly what at least 80 percent of all churches are doing; they major in getting people converted. On the contrary, Jesus said, "Go make *disciples.*" Jesus was trying to get people to understand how important discipline is. Discipline is the only way to experience genuine freedom—spiritually, emotionally, physically, and financially.

Live at Least Ten Percent Below Your Means

If you want to get out of debt, you have to live at least ten percent below your means. In other words, save ten percent of all your income. Most people, whether rich or broke, are guilty of either living at their means or living above their means. Both living above and at your means does not make good financial sense.

In fact, if you live at your means, you will eventually begin to live above your means simply because uncontrollable things will happen that will demand your finances. If you spend everything that comes in, how will you be able to pay for incidentals? You cannot. Hence, you will be forced to charge things all the time.

If you don't have money to pay for the charge now, how will you get it later? You won't. This kind of insanity will hold you in the cycle of debt. You might say, "I can't afford to save ten percent of my income." Actually you are paying out more, perhaps thirty or forty percent, because you won't save the measly ten percent.

What if your car breaks down today and you don't have the money to pay for it? You will be forced to charge the repairs on an interest-bearing credit card, which means that you will automatically pay far more for your repairs than you would have, had you the money saved. You might get a tax bill. Maybe you want to give to a charity. Perhaps you'll want to go on vacation. How about those family reunions? They cost money. You might also have to factor what it's going to cost to help you bum family members out. Costs add up quickly.

How about divorce? We are certainly not advocating divorce. But when it unfortunately happens, and it does, it's going to cost you. In fact, all the things I have mentioned cost money. And if you don't have anything saved toward them, they will put you deeper in the hole. If you have children in college, it's costing you money. Even if they have received scholarships for their education, you still have expenses, such as books, lodging, and food. (They do have to eat, you know.)

And let's not forget inflation. What college costs today will be far more in years to come. The average costs to attend Harvard University, Yale University, the University of Hartford, Stanford University, Pepperdine University, Brown University, or Princeton University are about $35,000 a year. If you have a newborn child today, the average price for those same institutions with inflation in mind will be $105,000 a year when he or she turns 18. That's just tuition. That does not include transportation, auto insurance, or food when your children get the munchies at night.

Do you have $105,000 in your hands right now to pay for one year of your child's college education? Four years will total more than $420,000. I hope you can see that saving ten percent of your income is just the start. You should be trying to save even more. Not saving ten percent of your income will force you into great debt.

You might say, "I'll save money just as soon as I get out of debt." I say, "Do them both simultaneously." If there were a major blizzard dumping from three to four feet of snow, would you wait to shovel after the storm was over? I would hope not. It would make far greater sense if you shoveled incrementally. It's better to take on a little at a time. Too much at one time will be tremendously overwhelming and burdensome. The synergy that is created by paying down your debts and saving at the same time will help you to reach your goal far sooner than if you waited.

Pay Twenty Percent More Than Your Regular Monthly Payment

Have you ever received a credit card bill asking you to pay less than ten dollars, even though you owe more than $1,000 on the card? If you have, I want you to know it's a trap. It's an outrage. It's a conspiracy to keep you forever their slave. If you owe $1,000 on your credit card, you will pay about $20 per month if your interest rate is 19.99 percent. If your interest charges are $20 and your monthly payment is only an affordable $10, your payment will never affect the principle balance.

You will pay on your credit card for eternity. In fact, you might be paying on your credit bills in Heaven at the rate you are going. So what's the solution? First, you must *always* pay more than your interest charges. Until you have paid on your interest, you will never affect the balance. So if your interest charges are $20, only the amount that you pay above $20 will be applied toward your principle. The credit card companies always get paid first, because they don't trust you. So they take their interest up front each month.

A rule of thumb is to always try and pay at least 20 percent more than your monthly payment. For example, if your monthly payment is $100, an additional $20 added to your payment will help to get you out of debt quicker than if you paid the minimum monthly payment required. If possible you should use this method with all your debt, including a house mortgage or car note. The 20-percent principle is one of the most effective ways to becoming debt free.

Budget Is Not a Bad Word

You need to give an account for every dollar you spend. You should know where your money is going and where your money has gone. If you are serious about debt freedom, you need to keep a ledger that lists all your expenses and monthly bills. You need to hold yourself accountable.

A few years ago, one of my parishioners who had a pre-existing drug problem was admitted to Dr. I.V. Hilliard's drug rehabilitation ministry at the Light Ministries in Houston, Texas. Unfortunately, he never finished the program and he is no longer attending our ministry. He had baulked that the program leaders did not want him to have any money on his person. Their proven theory was that most drug users do not give anyone an account for their spending. They earn money, and before the day is over, a large portion of their money has been spent on drugs. This is one of the main reasons why drug addicts stay on drugs. So their program stressed accountability.

You may not be a drug user, but you need to be accountable to someone for your spending. Whether you are unrestrained in your spending on clothes, cars, food, or drugs, it all gets you to the same place—nowhere and in debt. Obviously we all are accountable to God for our actions. However, you may need to ask someone who is qualified to help you set up a budget. Please don't cringe at the sound of the word *budget*. A budget helps you to become more sensible in your spending. A budget actually helps you to spend, save, and invest within the frame of what you have earned and no more.

If you earn only $500 weekly, why are your bills and expenses more than $600? In addition, you haven't factored in your savings plan for the week. You don't have anything to put aside. Why? You haven't budgeted. A budget helps you to accomplish your goals and provides the visual blueprint to see how it's going to happen for you. It also helps you to have something left over after the day is through.

However you get paid, divide your bills into that number. For example, if you get paid every week, then divide your monthly $100 electric bill by four (four weeks). So you are actually budgeting $25 toward your electric bill on a weekly basis. If you get paid twice a month, then divide the $100 by two, equaling $50, on so on. You should determine how much money you need in order to pay your expenses on a weekly, twice-a-month, or monthly basis.

Then you should list all your expenses and bills. Bills are particulars that can be paid off, such as credit card debt, mortgages, car loans, and so on. Expenses are continual costs that really never get paid in full because they are necessary to sustain human life. These consist of phone bills; electricity bills; heating bills (oil, gas or electric); water bills; auto, life, and health insurances; and property and car taxes.

Things such as cable and Internet bills are somewhat luxuries, not necessities. They are only considered needed items if either of them helps you to earn money. If they don't provide an opportunity for more income, then go to your local library to use the Internet if you need to. Drop by a friend's house if you really need to watch a cable broadcasted show. Eliminate anything from your budget that isn't necessary. Remember, debt freedom is your goal.

On page 117 is an example of a Bills and Expenses Ledger. You will need to tailor your own personal ledger to fit your particular situation. Remember that everything should be measured against your total income. You initially need to determine what your income is on a monthly, bi-weekly, or weekly basis. Then list every bill and expense you can think of. You want to have as accurate figures as possible.

> *Note: If the total amount you have budgeted is more than your monthly income, you will need to readjust your budgeted amounts based on those facts.

Tithing—A Sure Investment

As always, I like to save the best for last. If you are not a faithful tither, you are already in debt. Despite what you have been falsely taught concerning the tithe, you need to know that the tithe belongs to the Lord. I've always found it amusing when people say, "I can't afford to tithe." What they don't understand is that the tithe is not theirs to withhold. Do you tell the government, "I can't afford to pay taxes"? Of course you don't—even though in most cases that would be true because most people are taxed far more heavily than they can afford to pay. Yet they still pay up. The government takes their money first because they don't trust you to pay them. God, on the other hand, wants you to trust Him so much that you give not out of compulsion, but rather from a heart of *love*.

Tithing really is a matter of *love*. Out of your true love for God you tithe. When you don't, you cause the spirit of debt to overtake you. However, this is not God's will for your life. He wants you to live under an open Heaven so that He can pour out a blessing that you won't have room to receive. But if you don't tithe, this can never happen for you.

> *"Will a man rob God? Yet you have robbed Me! But you say, 'In what way have we robbed You?' In tithes and offerings. You are cursed with a curse, for you have robbed Me, even this whole nation. Bring all the tithes into the storehouse, that there may be food in My house, and try Me now in*

Bills and Expenses	Monthly Payment
Tithes (10% of your gross income)	
Offerings (This includes special offerings and missions giving)	
Income Taxes	
Savings and Investments	
Electric Bill	
Heating Bill	
Water Bill	
Telephone Bill	
Mortgage	
VISA	
AMEX	
Department Store Credit Cards	
Auto, Health, Property and Life Insurances	
Child Care Expense	
Food	
Clothing	
Gasoline	
Entertainment	
Car Loan	
Personal Loan	
Cable or Satellite Television Expense	
Internet Server	
Grand Total	This amount should be far less than your monthly take-home income.

this," says the Lord of hosts, "if I will not open for you the windows of heaven and pour out for you such blessing that there will not be room enough to receive it. And I will rebuke the devourer for your sakes, so that he will not destroy the fruit of your ground, nor shall the vine fail to bear fruit for you in the field," says the Lord of hosts; "and all nations will call you blessed, for you will be a delightful land," says the Lord of hosts (Malachi 3:8-12).

It sounds kind of silly to think that you can rob the God of the universe. It's not like you can go up to God with a gun and say, "Give me all Your money or else." That's not how we rob God. The Bible makes it very clear that God is the owner of everything that is living.

For every beast of the forest is Mine, and the cattle on a thousand hills. I know all the birds of the mountains, and the wild beasts of the field are Mine. "If I were hungry, I would not tell you; for the world is Mine, and all its fullness" (Psalm 50:10-12).

We know that God cannot lack nor can we diminish Him; He is God. We rob God when we refuse to tithe because God cannot bless us. He has established a way for us to be blessed when we obey His Word concerning tithes and offering. If we obey out of a heart of love, then we free God to bless our lives. If we disobey, then we chain the hands of God so that no matter how much He wants to bless us, He cannot. We prevent the hands of God from blessing us through our conscious ignoring of His Word.

The tithe represents ten percent of your income. If you want to be prosperous, always tithe to God first, then tithe to yourself. Live off the remaining 80 percent. That's not only the truth on breaking the back of the debt cycle but is also relevant to total life prosperity. Tithing to your local church really works. If you are being fed the Word of God through your ministry, you should tithe to that ministry out of a heart of love.

Getting Out of Debt

I'll never forget when I attended a book signing at the CBA (Christian Booksellers' Convention) in Atlanta, Georgia, in July 2000. I was there to sign books for my *Healing for the 21st Century* release. At this same convention was a man who had written and self-published a book about why the church of today should not tithe. He was giving copies away to people as they walked by.

Most people would not receive the book. I'm sure they were happy tithers and did not want to contaminate their theology with this man's foolish revelation. Interestingly, he was going from booth to booth trying to influence various publishers to publish his book. He explained that he did not have the money to print more than five hundred copies. He simply could not afford to publish his so-called "new revelation" message.

The Holy Spirit spoke to my heart and said, "That man is under a curse. He's so cursed that he can't even afford to publish the message that he believes is so true." I have always been under the conviction that if God gives you a message, He will bring the right people and contacts into your life to get the message published. God will pay for whatever He orders.

This man was obviously deceived. Yet his ignorance and rebellion caused him to live a lifestyle of need, want, and begging. That is not how God's people ought to live. That is not how you or I should live. I intend to have God on my side. More than anything, I desire God's favor upon my life. I sincerely believe that it will happen when I give my tithes.

Tithing is a lifeline. It is your connection to His Kingdom. It proves your love for God, His Church, and His people. It also shows that you are serious about being debt free and becoming wealthy. It starts with the tithe. You can commit to all sorts of investments mentioned in this book, but if you don't tithe, you will remain under a curse and your investments will eventually go sour. That's not a threat—it's a promise.

At *The Family of God*, the church I pastor in East Hartford, Connecticut, we confess the tither's creed every time we receive the tithes and offerings during our service. The Holy Bible teaches us that confession always brings possession. Since we have started using this confession during our offertory in worship services, our tithes and offerings have doubled.

I believe that if you use this same confession in your services, you will see major changes also. In fact, take it one step further. You should state this confession every day when you wake up and when you lay your head to rest. Let it become a natural part of you. Let tithing become something that is a part of your character, not just something you do every now and then.

The Tither's Creed

I am a tither. I bring my tithe to God's house faithfully, consistently, and honestly. Through my financial giving and my obedience to God's Word I help to establish God's Kingdom in the earth. It is my primary concern to ensure that the house of God will not lack in any area. I realize that God has empowered me to gain financial wealth. He will continue to prosper me as long as I do not forget to bless His house first. I stand in full agreement with God's Word that the blessing of good health, financial well-being, strong families, good relationships, and soundness of mind all belong to me because I choose to give the tithes and offering.

Get on the road to debt freedom and biblical blessings. Be a tither.

Endnote

1. Dorothy Winbush Riley, ed., *My Soul Looks Back, 'Less I Forget: A Collection of Quotations by People of Color* (New York: Harper Collins, 1993), 94.

Chapter Ten

A Totally Healthy You

Beloved, I pray that you may prosper in all things and be in health, just as your soul prospers (3 John 2).

This Scripture verse should be one that every Christian believer lives by. It should be your creed. You should believe without a doubt that it is God's greatest desire that you, His child, prosper in everything that you set your hand to, and He knows so well that you cannot prosper in everything that you set out to do if your health is defective.

God's desire is that you understand how to keep your house—your body and temple—in optimum shape. If you are serious about good health, you can't just put anything in your body and expect it to run well. Would you put rubbing alcohol in your car's gasoline tank? Instead of motor oil would you put cooking oil in your car engine? You probably think that sounds a bit silly. And it does. However, it is as equally silly for you to put just anything into your body when God has provided the right food for you to consume.

The Total Package

For the drunkard and the glutton shall come to poverty: and drowsiness shall clothe a man with rags (Proverbs 23:21 KJV).

Or do you not know that your body is the temple of the Holy Spirit who is in you, whom you have from God, and you are not your own? For you were bought at a price; therefore glorify God in your body and in your spirit, which are God's (1 Corinthians 6:19-20).

If you are a glutton, which means that you eat uncontrollably, not only will you have great health challenges, but you will also experience poverty. You may think, *I know a whole lot of people who are grossly overweight who are not poor.* That may be true. However, poverty comes in many forms. Maybe they are not experiencing financial poverty, yet they could be dealing with physical poverty. According to the Bible, if you suffer from such a condition, you are in no position to point the finger at someone who is an alcoholic. While an alcoholic has a problem with alcohol consumption, your problem may be food consumption. God does not see either problem as being different from the other.

Both problems will cause your temple (your body) to become defiled just as much as wanton living will. So if you are not in shape physically, this chapter is for you. If you believe that you are in perfect physical health, read on anyhow; I think you just might learn something valuable.

People always ask me, "Pastor Aaron, what should I eat? Is this food good for you? Is that food harmful?" Before I give you my commentary on what I have researched and live by, let me give you God's Word. His Word specifically lists what is good to eat and what is not good to eat. First, God encourages us to eat vegetation, things that grow from the ground. Fruits, herbs, and vegetables were created by God to help us live a disease-free life.

And God said, "See, I have given you every herb that yields seed which is on the face of all the earth, and every tree whose fruit yields seed; to you it shall be for food. Also, to every beast of the earth, to every bird of the air, and to everything that creeps on the earth, in which there is life, I have given every green herb for food"; and it was so (Genesis 1:29-30).

To Eat or Not to Eat?

Without adding or taking away, I want you to read what God's Word says. You may think that because this Scripture is in the Old Testament, it doesn't apply. Let me assure you that this is not just law, but common sense. By following these biblical guidelines, your health will improve drastically. On the other hand, if you don't follow these guidelines, God won't love you any less, nor will He punish you.

You will still get to Heaven in a timely fashion. These Scriptures are not given as a set of rules that you'll never be able to follow. Don't feel guilty. Just understand that all the words in the Bible are there for our benefit. *"All Scripture is given by inspiration of God, and is profitable for doctrine, for reproof, for correction, for instruction in righteousness, that the man of God may be complete, thoroughly equipped for every good work"* (2 Tim. 3:16-17).

Most pastors *never* teach from the Scriptures below. They teach on salvation, grace, and regeneration, but totally ignore entire chapters that they may not understand or just don't want to apply. I think it is an injustice to harp on one thing while totally ignoring a whole section of God's Word. If He allowed it to be in His Word, it must be there for a valid reason. Read, learn, grow, and live.

You shall not eat any detestable thing. These are the animals which you may eat: the ox, the sheep, the goat, the deer, the gazelle, the roe deer, the wild goat, the mountain goat, the antelope, and the mountain sheep. And you may eat every animal with cloven hooves, having the hoof split into two parts, and that chews the cud, among the animals. Nevertheless, of those that chew the cud or have cloven hooves, you shall not eat, such as these: the camel, the hare, and the rock hyrax; for they chew the cud but do not have cloven hooves; they are unclean for you. Also the swine is unclean for you, because it has cloven hooves, yet does not chew the cud; you shall not eat their flesh or touch their dead carcasses. These you may eat of all that are in the waters: you may eat all that have fins and scales. And whatever does not have fins and scales you shall not eat; it is unclean for you. All clean birds you may eat. But these you shall not eat: the eagle, the vulture, the buzzard, the red kite, the falcon, and the kite after their kinds; every raven after its kind; the ostrich, the short-eared owl, the sea gull, and the hawk after their kinds; the little owl, the screech owl, the white owl, the jackdaw, the carrion vulture, the fisher owl, the stork, the heron after its kind, and the hoopoe and the bat. Also every creeping thing that flies is unclean for you; they shall not be eaten. You may eat all clean birds. You shall not eat anything that dies of itself; you may give it to the alien who is within your gates, that he may eat it, or you may sell it to a foreigner; for you are a holy people to the Lord your God. You shall not boil a young goat in its mother's milk (Deuteronomy 14:3-21).

The Top Ten Foods to Avoid and Why

Billions of dollars are spent each year on diets. People seem to be in such a hurry to lose weight. Think about this: You were not born the weight that you are now. It took years for you to grow and develop into your present size. If you have gone past the size you think you should be, then you need to realize that it will take time to return to your desired weight.

Personally, I am totally opposed to the concept of diets and dieting. The first three letters of the word *diet* are d-i-e. That is exactly what most people feel like when they go on a diet; they feel like they are dying. My approach has always been to change the way I eat. There are some things I should avoid, and some things I should include in my overall eating plan. I believe that when you simply eat right and combine healthy eating with a regular exercise schedule, you will begin to see results that will last.

> "The first three letters of the word diet are d-i-e. That is exactly what most people feel like when they go on a diet; they feel like they are dying."

You must be extremely cautious not to try out every new diet that comes down the pike. The diets that offer overnight results should be avoided at all costs. Those are the diets that come complete with a casket and tombstone. Weight loss and weight control need to happen over a period of time. You should only expect to see weight change when you change what you choose to put into your mouth.

Don't believe it when you hear companies advertise, "Eat anything you want and still lose all the weight." I know that is what you want to hear, but it's simply not true. So-called miracle pills are not your solution but rather a temporary escape from an obligation to yourself to exercise godly discipline. I believe you can do it. You have to believe in yourself.

Following is a list of the top ten foods you should avoid if you want to lead a healthy life.

1. PIG—This is the number-one, nastiest animal that anyone can consume. Pigs were never created by God to be consumed by His people. Their purpose can be easily discovered when you visit a pigpen. They have been put on this earth to consume all the trash that we should not.

The Total Package

They eat trash, which includes but is not limited to, rotten stinking fecal material that breeds worms and maggot larva and parasites. They are moving, walking garbage disposals. When you eat any form of pork, you ingest trash and decomposing, rotting flesh and garbage into your veins. No wonder so many people in America live with diseased bodies. In addition, sodium nitrates are loaded into bacon products and are carcinogenic, or cancer causing. The best-known illness caused by a food-borne parasite is trichinosis. Trichinosis comes from eating undercooked pork. It is first transmitted to pigs when they are fed uncooked garbage or when infested rodents such as rats invade the hogs' feeding areas. I grew up eating all pork products (hot dogs, bacon, sausage, ham, pepperoni, pork chops, fat back, pork skins, ham hocks, chitterlings) and loved them. I was taught that eating meats and plenty of them were healthy. During my entire childhood and teenage years I was as sick as a pig. Needless to say, I was as fat as a pig too. When I came into the knowledge of the truth concerning pork during my early 20's, I immediately took it out of my eating plan forever. To my amazement, I lost 25 pounds in about three months just by excluding the pig. My healthiness increased literally by 100 percent after I made this quality decision. I'm convinced your health will improve greatly by making this change too.

2. Red Meat—Beef keeps you constipated. It takes an extremely long time to break down in your digestive system. It has been proven to contribute to prostate cancer because of its decaying attributes. It literally clogs your veins and arteries, which in turn slows down your blood flow, leading to heart disease and possible death. For

more information about the truth about beef, read Howard F. Lyman's *Mad Cowboy—The Plain Truth From the Cattle Rancher Who Won't Eat Meat*, published by Scribner, New York. Mr. Lyman appeared on the Oprah Winfrey Show in 1996 to discuss what actually goes on in the beef industry. The beef industry in turn sued Oprah Winfrey, but they were not successful. Lyman's book will inform you of what happens with the beef from the ranch to your plate.

3. Sodas, Powdered Drinks, and Non-Natural Juices— Many artificial drinks are loaded with sugar. Excessive amounts of sugar can lead to diabetes, teeth decay, and premature aging. There is no nutritive value whatsoever in soda. You should replace sodas and other non-natural juices with pure distilled water and all natural fruit juices.

4. High-Fat Dairy Products (Artificial Ice Cream and Milk)—High-fat dairy products contribute to allergies. This year I have noticed that allergies have been at a high all around the country. Dairy products worsen pre-existing allergy conditions and may even be the birthplace of allergies. Whole milk is not good for you and is not a natural source of calcium. Calcium is added to whole milk. I get more calcium in orange juice than I do from milk. Cows' milk is for cows. Unless you feel like a cow you may want to choose another alternative. Use soy milk instead of milk. It's made from naturally grown soy beans and is rich in protein.

5. Hydrogenated or Partially Hydrogenated Vegetable Oils (Margarine)—They clog your veins, making it difficult for blood to flow freely throughout your body.

6. Aspartame and other Artificial Sweeteners—These sweeteners are popping up everywhere. They were first disguised in *Nutra Sweet* and *Equal*. But since the food industry realized that most of their buyers don't like to read, they have no fear in listing aspartame as part of the ingredients without disguise. These sweeteners have been traced to the cause of brain tumors, migraine headaches, delirium, and brain cancer.

7. Fast Foods—Except for a very few, most fast-food chains help to kill you quickly. Well-cooked red meat is not healthy, but its health risk increases drastically if it is not prepared properly. There is no way you can serve billions of minute-made hamburgers and expect to do it in a healthy way. If you choose to eat beef, it must be properly cooked, always well done. If it is not, it will cause major problems in your health. What about mad cow disease?

   Since it was identified in the mid-1980s in Britain, mad cow disease, or BSE, has resulted in the slaughter of millions of cattle—and the deaths of dozens of people from the related brain-wasting disease known as vCJD. Mad cow scares have since spread across Europe as governments try to cope with possible infections and resultant fears.[1]

8. Processed Foods (including lunchmeats)— If something has to be processed in order for you to eat it, then it's probably not the best thing for you to put into your temple. Food needs to be prepared, not processed. Processed foods usually do not have any nutritive value. Basically, you are eating junk just to fill up a hole. It's like putting concrete in a hole in the ground and then expect something to grow out

of that hole. Processed lunchmeats, Twinkies, ding-dongs, cupcakes, chicken nuggets, fish sticks, instant noodles, some cheeses, and some deli meats are on the processed food hit list. Twinkies will last inside of its plastic wrapping for years because of its processing. It seems as if it has an embalming capability to it. Ready to be embalmed?

9. Caffeine Products—This is found in coffee, tea, and chocolate. It is a natural drug that stimulates the brain and the nervous system. Like any drug it is highly addictive. It can cause depression, headaches and heart-throbbing pains. When I was addicted to caffeine, I drank about seven 12-ounce cups of coffee each day. I shook all the time and had nervous twitches. Worse yet was when I quick the habit cold turkey. I broke out into a sweat and experienced muscle aching that was unusually painful. That experience alone convinced me never to touch the stuff again. In addition, overuse of caffeine is one of the major risk factors for hypertension.

10. Alcohol—Alcohol is fermented or rotten drink. It destroys human brain cells, stomach linings, and attacks your pancreas. It is the leading cause of sclerosis of the liver and promotes kidney failure and cancer. Alcoholism erodes your finances, promotes family divisions, causes you to act like a blooming idiot, and kills innocent people in car accidents. Need I say anymore?

The Top Four Foods to Include and Why

These foods are absolutely essential to good health. The lack of them may cause serious deficiencies and possible sickness in your body. Some of them have actually been proven to prevent cancer.

The Total Package

1. Water.

2. Vegetables—broccoli, brussel sprouts, cauliflower, celery, carrots, cabbage, squash, sweet potatoes, kale, radishes, onions, corn, spinach.

3. Fruits—cantaloupe, papaya, oranges, grapefruit, apples, watermelon, honeydew melon, bananas, strawberries, blueberries.

4. Grain—brown rice, wheat, oats, bran.

Vitamins, Minerals, and Herbs

It is impossible for your body to receive all the nutrients necessary for good health on a daily basis through eating. It is not humanly possible for you to eat everything that you need and get your proper daily allowance. Therefore, you need to take a supplement every day to help replenish and restore those vital nutrients that were lost.

I realize there are several thousand supplements on the market that you can take. Everybody's system is slightly different so there are some things you may need more than I need. However, I have listed some of the top supplements that benefit most people when they take them. You might call this list, "Pastor Aaron's Hot Ten List." Although this is not a comprehensive list, these are ten supplements that I have consistently taken for several years, which have helped me to enjoy impeccable health. I hope you experience similar results.

1. *A complete multi-vitamin* gives you a smorgasbord of the needed vitamins.

2. *Calcium* helps to keep your teeth and bones healthy and promotes a healthy heartbeat.

3. *Vitamin C* helps in lowering cholesterol, heals wounds and burns, helps to prevent various viral and bacterial

infections, protects against cancer-producing agents, acts as a natural laxative, strengthens cellular function, fights against allergy producers, and supports the immune system.

4. *Garlic* reduces blood pressure, thus preventing the risk of heart disease, fights infection, destroys some types of cancer cells, and relieves gas.

5. *Ginseng* helps the body adjust to stress, reduces cholesterol, enhances physical and mental performance, increases energy, and increases sexual desire.

6. *Chromium Picolinate* helps to regulate blood sugar levels, aids in the prevention of high blood pressure, and works against diabetes.

7. *Coq10* promotes a healthy heart; studies have shown that it aids in overall teeth and gum health.

8. *Ginkgo Biloba* improves blood circulation, improves mental and memory functions, and possibily retards the aging process; it may be helpful in the treatment of Alzheimer patients and may prevent some types of cancer.

9. *Psyllium* heals hemorrhoids, prevents heart disease, acts as a laxative, and is an excellent source of dietary fiber.

10. *Echinacea* is an overall immune system strengthener, prevents viral and bacteria infections, and aids against colds and flu.

An Exercise Plan That Fits You

For bodily exercise profits a little, but godliness is profitable for all things, having promise of the life that now is and of that which is to come (1 Timothy 4:8).

The Total Package

I have heard this Scripture used to justify lack of physical activity. This Scripture is actually not disapproving exercise but rather saying that physical exercise will not profit your spirit. However, it will profit your body. If you are physically able to do so, exercise is extremely helpful in maintaining good health and proper circulation.

There are so many exercises that you can do. One is not necessarily better than another. You have to find the exercise that best fits your body and your personal liking. I personally like to run. I run 26.2-mile marathons and enjoy them greatly. Other people tell me I am insane for doing so. You have got to do what works for you. The bottom line is that you have to do something. Be sure to consult your physician before starting any exercise program, particularly if you already have a preexisting condition. Try to exercise at least three times each week for half an hour.

Here is a list of what I consider the best overall exercises for your body:

1. Swimming.

2. Walking.

3. Running.

4. Weight Training.

5. Stretching.

Dehydrations Kills—Water Gives Life

Then the angel showed me the river of the water of life, as clear as crystal, flowing from the throne of God and of the Lamb (Revelation 22:1 NIV).

Water is second to oxygen in importance of all things that are necessary to sustain human life. Water can be found in all tissues including teeth, fat, bone, and muscle. Water is the medium of all body fluids such as blood, digestive fluids, lymph, urine, and perspiration. Water is a lubricant for saliva and mucus membranes. Water supplies the body with oxygen and vital nutrients.

Water is the most essential thing your body needs. Your body is 85 percent liquid. The human brain is 75 percent liquid. Just through breathing alone you lose about a quart of water each day. Water has the ability to cleanse your entire body and rid it of poisons, toxic material, and waste matter. *Your Body's Many Cries for Water* by F. Batmanghelidj, M.D. is a must read for anyone who desires to understand just how important water is.

His book details how water is the cure to most maladies of the body. He gives detailed yet controversial research describing how people would not have to take many of the medications that they take if they only increased their water intake. He suggests that water can help to prevent and reverse the aging process. It will eliminate heartburn, back pains, arthritis, colitis pain, anginal pain, and migraine headaches.

He proves that water has the components that can cure asthma in a short amount of time. He also proves that you can lose weight naturally and without effort by increasing your water intake. He says most people are really not sick, as some medical doctors would convince them to believe; they are dehydrated. Dr. Batmanghelidj's book is published through Global Health Solutions. You may contact him on the web at www.watercure.com.

Colon Cleansing

Colon hydrotherapy is a safe and effective method of removing waste from the large intestine without the use of drugs. It is a cleansing process where warm-filtered water is put inside of the colon through a rectal tube inserted into the rectum. The waste is softened and loosened, resulting in evacuation through natural peristalsis. This process is repeated between three to six times during a session

The Total Package

depending on the person. Before you start feeling uncomfortable about the process, let me assure you that most people find this process a pleasant and soothing experience.

Most diseases originate in the colon. One of the main degenerative diseases of the colon is colon cancer. This disease can be successfully prevented through proper nutrition, exercise, getting screened, and keeping the colon walls clean. Several years ago there was a man who had a colostomy, a surgical procedure where the anus is removed as well as the diseased portion of the intestines. In other words, once this process is completed, you cannot eliminate waste by normal process but rather are confined to eliminating your waste in a plastic bag that is attached to the your abdomen.

Trying to matriculate back into normal life after his surgery, this man went for a job interview. During his interview his waste bag fell off, and the fecal contents of the bag fell on the floor. The smell of the waste was horrid. He was so embarrassed by this incident that he went home and shot himself in the head. As drastic as this may seem, it is a true story.

Your intestines do not have a self-cleaning mechanism. You have to intentionally do things that will keep your colon clean. When your colon is clean your intestinal walls will be better able to extract the vitamins and nutrients from the food you eat, giving you an optimum feeling and performance. You should have this procedure performed by someone who is a certified colon hydro-therapist. To find out more about colon care, read Dr. Norman W. Walker's *Colon Health: The Key to a Vibrant Life,* published by Norwalk Press.

God Breathed the Breath of Life

And the Lord God formed man of the dust of the ground, and breathed into his nostrils the breath of life; and man became a living being (Genesis 2:7).

Clean air and proper breathing are the single most important factors to your good health. Unfortunately, we do not have much control over our air supply and the pollutants that fill the air. In major cities around the United States the air is constantly being contaminated by smog, car exhaust, industrial waste, and chemical experimentation. Consequently, there is a major battle to continually keep the air clean in our communities.

It is still necessary however to practice breathing exercises several times each day primarily to get the oxygen flowing to and from your lungs. At least five times every day, I take time to breath deeply in, hold it, and then let it out. I hold my breath for at least five seconds before I exhale. I do this ten times each set. By doing this I am increasing the flow of oxygen to my body and to my brain.

It is very interesting that after God made man, He breathed life into him. That breath represents the essence of who we are. Without it or with a limited supply of it, we will die. I encourage you to travel to areas within the United States that are not so inundated with industrial life and that are not densely populated. In these types of regions take advantage of the fresh air supply and the natural outdoors, and use this time to recharge and fill up on the source of life—God's breath.

Pastor Aaron's Recommended Health and Healing Reading

Maximum Energy, Siloam Press—Ted Broer

The Bible Cure, Creation House—Reginald Cherry, M.D.

Walking in Divine Health, Siloam Press—Don Colbert, M.D

Moses Wasn't Fat, Axion Publications—Tom Ciola

Healing for the 21ˢᵗ Century, Whitaker House—Aaron D. Lewis

Flood the Body With Oxygen: Therapy for Our Polluted World, Energy Publications—Ed McCabe

Earl Mindell's Vitamin Bible, Warner Books—Earl Mindell

The Total Package

Earl Mindell's Herb Bible, Fireside—Earl Mindell

Garlic, The Miracle Nutrient, Keats—Earl Mindell

Eating for Optimum Health, Knopf—Andrew Weil, M.D.

Endnote

1. "Mad Cow Disease: Counting the Cost." *CNN.com/In-Depth Specials*. Cable News Network, 2000. June 12, 2003. <www.cnn.com/specials/2000/mad cow/>.

Chapter Eleven

Lessons from a Lazy Man

For the kingdom of heaven is like a man traveling to a far country, who called his own servants and delivered his goods to them. And to one he gave five talents, to another two, and to another one, to each according to his own ability; and immediately he went on a journey. Then he who had received the five talents went and traded with them, and made another five talents. And likewise he who had received two gained two more also. But he who had received one went and dug in the ground, and hid his lord's money. After a long time the lord of those servants came and settled accounts with them. So he who had received five talents came and brought five other talents, saying, "Lord, you delivered to me five talents; look, I have gained five more talents besides them." His lord said to him, "Well done, good and faithful servant; you were faithful over a few things, I will make you ruler over many things. Enter into the joy of your lord." He also who had received two talents came and said, "Lord, you delivered to me two talents; look, I have

137

gained two more talents besides them." His lord said to him, "Well done, good and faithful servant; you have been faithful over a few things, I will make you ruler over many things. Enter into the joy of your lord." Then he who had received the one talent came and said, "Lord, I knew you to be a hard man, reaping where you have not sown, and gathering where you have not scattered seed. And I was afraid, and went and hid your talent in the ground. Look, there you have what is yours." But his lord answered and said to him, "You wicked and lazy servant, you knew that I reap where I have not sown, and gather where I have not scattered seed. So you ought to have deposited my money with the bankers, and at my coming I would have received back my own with interest. Therefore take the talent from him, and give it to him who has ten talents. For to everyone who has, more will be given, and he will have abundance; but from him who does not have, even what he has will be taken away. And cast the unprofitable servant into the outer dark-ness. There will be weeping and gnashing of teeth" (Matthew 25:14-30).

The parable of the talents shares one of the greatest lessons in the Bible on the importance of investing. One of the first things to gather from this narrative is God gives each person what he or she can handle in life, or in other words, *to each according to his or her own ability.* This is a very significant truth. God will never give you more than you can handle.

On the other hand, God will not shortchange you by giving to you so little that even if you have invested what little He gave you, it would not make a tangible difference. God always gives enough to provide us with an advantage in life. He always gives us enough raw materials that, once properly utilized, will create an industry that will support others and ourselves.

Lessons from a Lazy Man

There are three men in this text. Each man has distinctively different abilities. Some investors are savvier than others, just as some craftsmen are more skilled than others in their prospective fields. Although there is a difference between a finish carpenter and a framing carpenter, both are equally carpenters. In the same way, each of these three men were expected to produce and intellectually capable of producing a profit from their investment strategies.

"God always gives enough to provide us with an advantage in life."

If each man did not know how to invest, then the choice to not invest would not have bore such stringent consequences. Even if one of the three did not have the proper training to multiply his seed, he could have always asked one of the others who were also charged with the duty of governing their master's money. The point is if their master commanded these men to make a profit and provided all of them with the start-up cost to do so, none of them should have had an excuse as to why he could not perform this simple task.

As the story goes, one man was given five talents, the other three, and the other one. When the master returned from his journey, the man who had been given five talents doubled his profit ,earning him five additional talents. The one who had been given three earned three more. They both doubled their profits and pleased the master. The man who had been given one talent did not do anything with his lord's money. Do you feel there are times when you do nothing with the gifts, talents, finances, or resources that God has entrusted you with?

There were many things that he could have done with the talent, but he chose, like so many of us, to do absolutely nothing. What kind of consequences do you suppose a person should suffer for simply doing nothing? It would be most logical to witness the punishment of a person who perpetrated a criminal act. If he consciously violated another person in some sort of way, it would be understandable why he would have to bear the burden of his thoughtless actions.

But this man did not do anything. which leads us to the point that his crime was not centered on stealing, killing, or even putting other gods before Yahweh. His crime was doing nothing. Can you imagine spending your life behind bars because you did nothing? This was the case with the one-talent man in this passage.

God tends to see things differently from the way we do. The people whom we may set free, God may incarcerate. The people whom God gives liberty to, we often place in bondage. However the case, God is always righteous and just. This simply means that if God chooses to do something, whether we see the relevance in the matter or not is inconsequential. God does what He does because He is always right.

When this man was asked to give an account for his stewardship, he came up empty. He could not even produce the initial investment, for he had buried it away. His punishment was being cast into outer darkness where there was weeping and gnashing of teeth. This man went to hell for not making a profit. Knowing that alone should make you more profit-conscious in life. This one-talent man made an excuse, but it did not suffice.

Could it be that you have allowed yourself to live in an earthly hell because you have not used what you already have? Have you complained to God and charged Him with injustice and unfair treatment simply because you believe that other people have been given so much more in life? "If only I were given more, life would be so much better," you say. This story is one of helpful instruction.

God has given you enough to start with in life. If you desire more, you will have to prove you can properly manage what you were first given. After you have proven yourself on that level, you will be able to go to the next level. With new levels of affluence, influence, and health, there will always be greater levels of responsibility. You cannot expect to become gold without first going through the process of pressurization and intense heating.

You have been given two precious commodities—wealth and health, the latter being the greater. If you take care of and increase your present wealth and health, you will inevitably receive more. If you willfully choose to ignore the acres of diamonds that God has already entrusted you with, you should never expect to receive an increase. Hence, you will always live your life feeling robbed by those who have more substance than you have, thus continuing the aphorism—the rich get richer and the poor get poorer.

By using what you have already and starting now, you can reinvent the future that the enemy has attempted to ruin. You can have *The Total Package*. I sincerely trust that through these pages you have re-viewed yourself in a whole different light. I pray that you can grasp the reality of living a life that you previously thought was an impossibility. The truth is, the life you thought was reserved for the rich and famous in our world was actually reserved for you. Open your package!

The Total Package

George B. Thompson is a nationally recognized financial expert who has won numerous top sales awards and is the author of *Millionaires in Training: The Wealth Builder.*

Known for his passionate delivery style, dynamic charismatic energy, and practical message, Thompson is dedicated to empowering individuals with wealth building skills. He is a widely sought-after expert who has enriched the skills of thousand of executives, managers, and professionals at churches and non-profit companies all over the world.

George B. Thompson is a member of West Angeles Church of God in Christ, where the renowned Bishop Charles E. Blake serves as pastor. He holds a Bachelor of Arts degree in Business Communications from Pepperdine University and a Personal Financial Planning Designation from University of California, Los Angeles.

Pastor Aaron D. Lewis is one of our nation's great writers and critical thinkers on spiritual thought. With his wife, Tiwanna, he pastors a unique ministry, *The Family of God,* headquartered in East Hartford, Connecticut. Lewis has also distinguished himself as a leading healing minister, having held numerous healing crusades, revivals, conferences, and seminars in various parts of the United States.

Prior to his clerical journey Lewis invested more than nine years of his life as a professional salesperson and president and CEO of a major corporation. He teaches through his varied seminars, *Crossing the Red Sea to Be Debt Free* and *How to Create Financial Wealth,* spiritual secrets of the wealthy. Through his *Keys to Unlocking Your Destiny Seminars* Lewis is equally committed to ushering people from average lifestyles into the center of their God-given destinies.

A consummate writer, Aaron D. Lewis has written more than a half dozen books, which includes *Healing for the 21st Century,* a stellar book on how to receive divine healing, and *Keys to Unlocking Your Destiny,* a work that helps people discover their God-given purpose and assignment in life. He is also a contributing author to the best-selling series, *God Allows U-Turns,* edited by Allison Gappa Bottke. When Lewis is not writing or facilitating seminars around the country, you will find him completing 26.2-mile marathons or simply having family fun with his wife and five growing children.

OTHER BOOKS BY THE AUTHORS

Aaron D. Lewis
The Prince of Preachers: Listen to the Voice
Healing for the 21st Century
Keys to Unlocking Your Destiny

George B. Thompson
Millionaires in Training: The Wealth Builder